T0294086

THE PEN OF GLORY

BAHÁ'U'LLÁH

THE PEN
OF GLORY

BAHÁ'U'LLÁH

Bahá'í
PUBLISHING
Wilmette, Illinois

Bahá'í Publishing, Wilmette, IL 60091

20 19 18 17   4 3 2 1

Library of Congress Cataloging-in-Publication Data
Names: Bahá'u'lláh, 1817–1892, author.
Title: The pen of glory : selected works of Bahá'u'lláh.
Description: Wilmette, IL : Bahá'í Publishing, 2017. | Originally
    published: 2008. | Includes bibliographical references and index.
Identifiers: LCCN 2016052705 (print) | LCCN 2017004787 (ebook)
| ISBN
    9781618511195 (alk. paper) | ISBN 9781618511218 (ebook)
Subjects: LCSH: Bahai Faith—Doctrines.
Classification: LCC BP362 .A3 2017 (print) | LCC BP362 (ebook) |
DDC
    297.9/3822—dc23
LC record available at https://lccn.loc.gov/2016052705

Cover design by Andrew Johnson
Book design by Patrick J. Falso

CONTENTS

INTRODUCTION

The ministry of Bahá'u'lláh, the Prophet-Founder of the Bahá'í Faith, began during His imprisonment, in 1852, in a notorious dungeon known as the "Black Pit" and finally ended forty years later, after a series of successive banishments, with His passing in a remote outpost of the Ottoman empire. Despite the sufferings He endured and despite vehement opposition to His teachings on the part of governments and clergy, the attempts to silence Bahá'u'lláh or prevent the spread of His teachings were entirely unsuccessful. Over the course of His life He revealed a body of writings, unprecedented in religious history in both its scope and magnitude, that offers stunning articulations of God's will for humanity in this day.

Throughout His life Bahá'u'lláh was renowned for His divine wisdom and was sought out by many who desired access to His matchless insight. Indeed, many of Bahá'u'lláh's best-known works were originally written as epistles in which He embedded timeless lessons and unraveled questions that had perplexed generations. Among these effusions from Bahá'u'lláh's mighty pen are the several Tablets brought together in this volume, which includes a lengthy Arabic treatise known as the Javáhiru'l-Asrár (meaning literally the "gems" or "essences" of mysteries) as well as a number of Tablets addressed to individuals of Zoroastrian background, who were among the first outside the Islamic community to be attracted to His teachings.

In a prefatory note written above the opening lines of the original manuscript of the Javáhiru'l-Asrár, Bahá'u'lláh states,

> This treatise was written in reply to a seeker who had asked how the promised Mihdí could have become transformed into 'Alí-Muḥammad (the Báb). The opportunity provided by this question was seized to elaborate on a number of subjects, all of which are of use and benefit both to them that seek and to those who have attained, could ye perceive with the eye of divine virtue.

The "seeker" to whom Bahá'u'lláh alludes was Siyyid Yúsuf-i-Sihdihí Iṣfáhání, an Islámic notable, who at the time was residing in Karbilá. His questions were presented to Bahá'u'lláh through an intermediary, and this Tablet was revealed in response on the same day.

One of its central themes, Bahá'u'lláh indicates, is that of "transformation," meaning here the return of the Promised One of Islám in a different human guise. A number of other important themes are addressed in this work as well: the cause of the rejection of the Prophets of the past; the danger of a literal reading of scripture; the meaning of the signs and portents of the Bible concerning the advent of the new Manifestation of God; the continuity of divine revelation; intimations of Bahá'u'lláh's own approaching declaration; the significance of such symbolic terms as "the Day of Judgment," "the Resurrection," "attainment to the Divine Presence," and "life and death"; and the stages of the spiritual quest through "the Garden of Search," "the City of Love and Rapture," "the City of Divine Unity," "the Garden of Wonderment," "the City of Absolute Nothingness," "the City of Immortality," and "the City that hath no name or description."

Also presented here is Bahá'u'lláh's Tablet to Mánik-chí Limjí Hataria (1813–1890), also known as Mánikchí (Manekji) Ṣáḥib. Born in India of Zoroastrian parents, he was an able diplomat and devoted adherent of his ancestral religion. In 1854 he was appointed as an emissary on behalf of the Parsees of India to assist their coreligionists in Iran, who were suffering under the repressive policies of the Qájár monarchs. Some time after this he attained the presence of Bahá'u'lláh in Baghdád. Although maintaining to the end of his life allegiance to his Zoroastrian faith, he was attracted to the teachings of the new religion and, moved by the sacrifice of its early martyrs, became a lifelong admirer. Years after their meeting, he posed a series of questions to Bahá'u'lláh that led to the revelation of two Tablets of far-reaching significance, the first of which was sent to him in 1878.

The first Tablet, known as the Lawḥ-i-Mánikchí Ṣáḥib, is celebrated for its striking and well-known passages epitomizing the universality of Bahá'u'lláh's prophetic claim. Revealed in pure Persian at Mánikchí Ṣáḥib's bold request, the Tablet responds to the questions he had raised and proclaims some of the central tenets of the Faith of Bahá'u'lláh: "Be anxiously concerned with the needs of the age ye live in, and center your deliberations on its exigencies and requirements." "Turn your faces from the darkness of estrangement to the effulgent light of the daystar of unity." "Ye are the fruits of one tree, and the leaves of one branch." "Whatsoever leadeth to the decline of ignorance and the increase of knowledge hath been, and will ever remain, approved in the sight of the Lord of creation."

As inferred from the contents of a second Tablet, Mánikchí Ṣáḥib was not entirely satisfied with this reply, having anticipated a more expansive discussion of his specific questions. Bahá'u'lláh's further reply is contained in a lengthy Tablet, revealed on July 1, 1882, in the voice of His amanuensis Mírzá Áqá Ján. The Tablet is addressed to the eminent Bahá'í scholar Mírzá Abu'l-Faḍl, who at the time was employed as the personal secretary of Mánikchí Ṣáḥib, but a lengthy portion of it addresses the latter's questions. Bahá'u'lláh states at the outset that Mánikchí Ṣáḥib had "failed to consider the matter closely, for otherwise he would have readily admitted that not a single point was omitted," and explains that out of wisdom his questions had not been directly answered, but that even so, "the answers were provided in a language of marvelous concision and clarity." Throughout the remainder of the Tablet, the text of each of Mánikchí Ṣáḥib's questions is successively quoted, and detailed replies are given to each, in some cases connecting the questions to the universal principles enunciated in the previous Tablet.

The Tablet is noteworthy for its discussion of a range of questions regarding the tenets of both Abrahamic and non-Abrahamic religions, as understood by Mánikchí Ṣáḥib, including the nature of creation, the connection between faith and reason, the reconciliation of the differences that exist among the laws and ordinances of various religions, their respective claims to exclusivity, and their differing degrees of eagerness to welcome others into their fold. Bahá'u'lláh's responses emphasize that which is right and true in the various doctrines and beliefs under examination, rather than discarding them outright for inaccuracy or insufficiency.

Also included here are the Lawḥ-i-Haft Pursish (Tablet of the Seven Questions), which was addressed to Ustád Javán-Mard, a prominent early Bahá'í of Zoroastrian background and former student of Mánikchí Ṣáḥib, and two other Tablets also revealed to believers of the same origin. Together, the five Tablets to individuals of Zoroastrian background offer a glimpse of Bahá'u'lláh's love for, and special relationship with, the followers of a religion that had arisen many centuries earlier in the same land that witnessed the birth of His own Faith.

A word should perhaps be said about the literary style of English translations included herein. Bahá'u'lláh possessed a superlative command of classical Persian and Arabic, which He used as an instrument of transformative effect. His translators faced a daunting challenge,* for their rendering had not only to convey precisely the Author's intent but also to capture for the English reader the exalted and emotive spirit in which this intent was communicated. The

---

* A portion of the Lawḥ-i-Mánikchí Ṣáḥib and several excerpts from the other Tablets were previously translated by Shoghi Effendi; these have been incorporated into the text of the translations and listed in the appendix.

form of expression settled upon—faithful in both respects to the original—is reminiscent of that used by seventeenth-century translators of the Bible, unique in its perennial power to touch the soul.

Just as the body of adherents to Bahá'u'lláh's Cause has grown in the past century and a half, so too has a world-wide appreciation of the depth and import of His teachings. Though only a small portion of Bahá'u'lláh's writings has thus far been translated into English, the compiled works in this volume further contribute to Western readers' access to and appreciation of Bahá'u'lláh's magnificent outpouring of guidance for the collective coming-of-age of humankind.

THE PEN
OF GLORY

BAHÁ'U'LLÁH

1
GEMS OF DIVINE MYSTERIES

The essence of the divine mysteries
in the journeys of ascent set forth for those
who long to draw nigh unto God,
the Almighty, the Ever-Forgiving—blessed
be the righteous that quaff from
these crystal streams!

HE IS THE EXALTED,
THE MOST HIGH!

O thou who treadest the path of justice and beholdest the countenance of mercy! Thine epistle was received, thy question was noted, and the sweet accents of thy soul were heard from the inmost chambers of thy heart. Whereupon the clouds of the Divine Will were raised to rain upon thee the outpourings of heavenly wisdom, to divest thee of all that thou hadst acquired aforetime, to draw thee from the realms of contradiction unto the retreats of oneness, and to lead thee to the sacred streams of His Law. Perchance thou mayest quaff therefrom, repose therein, quench thy thirst, refresh thy soul, and be numbered with those whom the light of God hath guided aright in this day. 1.1

Encompassed as I am at this time by the dogs of the earth and the beasts of every land, concealed as I remain in the hidden habitation of Mine inner Being, forbidden as I may be from divulging that which God hath bestowed upon Me of the wonders of His knowledge, the gems of His wisdom, and the tokens of His power, yet am I loath to frustrate the hopes of one who hath approached the sanctuary of grandeur, sought to enter within the precincts of eternity, and aspired to soar in the immensity of this creation at the dawning of the divine decree. I shall therefore relate unto 1.2

thee certain truths from among those which God hath vouchsafed unto Me, this only to the extent that souls can bear and minds endure, lest the malicious raise a clamor or the dissemblers hoist their banners. I implore God to graciously aid Me in this, for unto such as beseech Him, He is the All-Bounteous, and of those who show mercy, He is the Most Merciful.

1.3 Know then that it behooveth thine eminence to ponder from the outset these questions in thy heart: What hath prompted the divers peoples and kindreds of the earth to reject the Apostles whom God hath sent unto them in His might and power, whom He hath raised up to exalt His Cause and ordained to be the Lamps of eternity within the Niche of His oneness? For what reason have the people turned aside from them, disputed about them, risen against and contended with them? On what grounds have they refused to acknowledge their apostleship and authority, nay, denied their truth and reviled their persons, even slaying or banishing them?

1.4 O thou who hast set foot in the wilderness of knowledge and taken abode within the ark of wisdom! Not until thou hast grasped the mysteries concealed in that which We shall relate unto thee canst thou hope to attain to the stations of faith and certitude in the Cause of God and in those who are the Manifestations of His Cause, the Daysprings of His Command, the Treasuries of His revelation, and the Repositories of His knowledge. Shouldst thou fail in this, thou wouldst be numbered with them that have not striven for the Cause of God, nor inhaled the fragrance of faith from the raiment of certitude, nor scaled the heights of the divine unity, nor yet recognized the stations of divine singleness within the Embodiments of praise and the Essences of sanctity.

Strive then, O My brother, to apprehend this matter, 1.5
that the veils may be lifted from the face of thy heart and
that thou mayest be reckoned among them whom God hath
graced with such penetrating vision as to behold the most
subtle realities of His dominion, to fathom the mysteries
of His kingdom, to perceive the signs of His transcendent
Essence in this mortal world, and to attain a station wherein
one seeth no distinction amongst His creatures and findeth
no flaw in the creation of the heavens and the earth.[1]

Now that the discourse hath reached this exalted and 1.6
intractable theme and touched upon this sublime and
impenetrable mystery, know that the Christian and Jewish
peoples have not grasped the intent of the words of God
and the promises He hath made to them in His Book, and
have therefore denied His Cause, turned aside from His
Prophets, and rejected His proofs. Had they but fixed their
gaze upon the testimony of God itself, had they refused to
follow in the footsteps of the abject and foolish among their
leaders and divines, they would doubtless have attained to
the repository of guidance and the treasury of virtue, and
quaffed from the crystal waters of life eternal in the city
of the All-Merciful, in the garden of the All-Glorious, and
within the inner reality of His paradise. But as they have
refused to see with the eyes wherewith God hath endowed
them, and desired things other than that which He in His
mercy had desired for them, they have strayed far from the
retreats of nearness, have been deprived of the living waters
of reunion and the wellspring of His grace, and have lain as
dead within the shrouds of their own selves.

Through the power of God and His might, I shall now 1.7
relate certain passages revealed in the Books of old, and
mention some of the signs heralding the appearance of the

Manifestations of God in the sanctified persons of His chosen Ones, that thou mayest recognize the Dayspring of this everlasting morn and behold this Fire that blazeth in the Tree which is neither of the East nor of the West.[2] Perchance thine eyes may be opened upon attaining the presence of thy Lord and thy heart partake of the blessings concealed within these hidden treasuries. Render thanks then unto God, Who hath singled thee out for this grace and Who hath numbered thee with them that are assured of meeting their Lord.

1.8   This is the text of that which was revealed aforetime in the first Gospel, according to Matthew, regarding the signs that must needs herald the advent of the One Who shall come after Him. He saith: "And woe unto them that are with child, and to them that give suck in those days. . ."[3] until the mystic Dove, singing in the midmost heart of eternity, and the celestial Bird, warbling upon the Divine Lote-Tree, saith: "Immediately after the oppression of those days shall the sun be darkened, and the moon shall not give her light, and the stars shall fall from heaven, and the powers of the heavens shall be shaken: and then shall appear the sign of the Son of man in heaven: and then shall all the tribes of the earth mourn, and they shall see the Son of man coming in the clouds of heaven with power and great glory. And he shall send his angels with a great sound of a trumpet."[4]

1.9   In the second Gospel, according to Mark, the Dove of holiness speaketh in such terms: "For in those days shall be affliction, such as was not from the beginning of the creation which God created unto this time, neither shall be."[5] And it singeth later with the same melodies as before, without change or alteration. God, verily, is a witness unto the truth of My words.

And in the third Gospel, according to Luke, it is recorded: 1.10
"There shall be signs in the sun, and in the moon, and in the
stars, and upon the earth distress of nations, with perplex-
ity; the sea and the waves roaring; and the powers of heaven
shall be shaken. And then shall they see the Son of man
coming in a cloud with power and great glory. And when
these things begin to come to pass, know that the kingdom
of God hath drawn nigh."[6]

And in the fourth Gospel, according to John, it is recorded: 1.11
"But when the Comforter is come, whom I will send unto
you from the Father, even the Spirit of truth, which proceedeth from the Father, he shall testify of me: and ye also shall
bear witness."[7] And elsewhere He saith: "But the Comforter,
which is the Holy Ghost, whom the Father will send in my
name, he shall teach you all things, and bring all things to
your remembrance, whatsoever I have said unto you."[8] And:
"But now I go my way to him that sent me; and none of
you asketh me, Whither goest thou? But because I have said
these things unto you . . ."[9] And yet again: "Nevertheless I
tell you the truth: It is expedient for you that I go away: for
if I go not away, the Comforter will not come unto you;
but if I depart, I will send him unto you."[10] And: "Howbeit
when he, the Spirit of truth, is come, he will guide you into
all truth: for he shall not speak of himself; but whatsoever he
shall hear, that shall he speak: and he will show you things
to come."[11]

Such is the text of the verses revealed in the past. By Him 1.12
besides Whom there is none other God, I have chosen to
be brief, for were I to recount all the words that have been
sent down unto the Prophets of God from the realm of His
supernal glory and the kingdom of His sovereign might,

all the pages and tablets of the world would not suffice to exhaust My theme. References similar to those mentioned, nay even more sublime and exalted, have been made in all the Books and Scriptures of old. Should it be My wish to recount all that hath been revealed in the past, I would most certainly be able to do so by virtue of that which God hath bestowed upon Me of the wonders of His knowledge and power. I have, however, contented Myself with that which was mentioned, lest thou become wearied in thy journey or feel inclined to turn back, or lest thou be overtaken by sadness and sorrow and overcome with despondency, trouble and fatigue.

1.13 Be fair in thy judgment and reflect upon these exalted utterances. Inquire, then, of those who lay claim to knowledge without a proof or testimony from God, and who remain heedless of these days wherein the Orb of knowledge and wisdom hath dawned above the horizon of Divinity, rendering unto each his due and assigning unto all their rank and measure, as to what they can say concerning these allusions. Verily, their meaning hath bewildered the minds of men, and that which they conceal of the consummate wisdom and latent knowledge of God even the most sanctified souls have been powerless to uncover.

1.14 Should they say: "These words are indeed from God, and have no interpretation other than their outward meaning," then what objection can they raise against the unbelievers among the people of the Book? For when the latter saw the aforementioned passages in their Scriptures and heard the literal interpretations of their divines, they refused to recognize God in those who are the Manifestations of His unity, the Exponents of His singleness, and the Embodiments of

His sanctity, and failed to believe in them and submit to their authority. The reason was that they did not see the sun darken, or the stars of heaven fall to the ground, or the angels visibly descend upon the earth, and hence they contended with the Prophets and Messengers of God. Nay, inasmuch as they found them at variance with their own faith and creed, they hurled against them such accusations of imposture, folly, waywardness, and misbelief as I am ashamed to recount. Refer to the Qur'án, that thou mayest find mention of all this and be of them that understand its meaning. Even to this day do these people await the appearance of that which they have learned from their doctors and imbibed from their divines. Thus do they say: "When shall these signs be made manifest, that we may believe?" But if this be the case, how could ye refute their arguments, invalidate their proofs, and challenge them concerning their faith and their understanding of their Books and the sayings of their leaders?

And should they reply: "The Books that are in the hands 1.15 of this people, which they call the Gospel and attribute to Jesus, the Son of Mary, have not been revealed by God and proceed not from the Manifestations of His Self," then this would imply a cessation in the abounding grace of Him Who is the Source of all grace. If so, God's testimony to His servants would have remained incomplete and His favor proven imperfect. His mercy would not have shone resplendent, nor would His grace have overshadowed all. For if at the ascension of Jesus His Book had likewise ascended unto heaven, then how could God reprove and chastise the people on the Day of Resurrection, as hath been written by the Imáms of the Faith and affirmed by its illustrious divines?

1.16   Ponder then in thine heart: Matters being such as thou dost witness, and as We also witness, where canst thou flee, and with whom shalt thou take refuge? Unto whom wilt thou turn thy gaze? In what land shalt thou dwell and upon what seat shalt thou abide? In what path shalt thou tread and at what hour wilt thou find repose? What shall become of thee in the end? Where shalt thou secure the cord of thy faith and fasten the tie of thine obedience? By Him Who revealeth Himself in His oneness and Whose own Self beareth witness to His unity! Should there be ignited in thy heart the burning brand of the love of God, thou wouldst seek neither rest nor composure, neither laughter nor repose, but wouldst hasten to scale the highest summits in the realms of divine nearness, sanctity, and beauty. Thou wouldst lament as a soul bereaved and weep as a heart filled with longing. Nor wouldst thou repair to thy home and abode unless God would lay bare before thee His Cause.

1.17   O thou who hast soared to the realm of guidance and ascended to the kingdom of virtue! Shouldst thou desire to apprehend these celestial allusions, to witness the mysteries of divine knowledge, and to become acquainted with His all-encompassing Word, then it behooveth thine eminence to inquire into these and other questions pertaining to thine origin and ultimate goal from those whom God hath made to be the Wellspring of His knowledge, the Heaven of His wisdom, and the Ark of His mysteries. For were it not for those effulgent Lights that shine above the horizon of His Essence, the people would know not their left hand from their right, how much less could they scale the heights of the inner realities or probe the depths of their subtleties! We beseech God therefore to immerse us in these surging seas, to grace us with the presence of these life-bearing breezes, and to cause us to abide in these divine and lofty precincts. Perchance we may divest ourselves of all that we have taken from each other and strip ourselves of such borrowed garments as we have stolen from our fellow men, that He may attire us instead with the robe of His mercy and the raiment of His guidance, and admit us into the city of knowledge.

Whosoever entereth this city will comprehend every science before probing into its mysteries and will acquire from the leaves of its trees a knowledge and wisdom encompassing such mysteries of divine lordship as are enshrined within the treasuries of creation. Glorified be God, its Creator and Fashioner, above all that He hath brought forth and ordained therein! By God, the Sovereign Protector, the Self-Subsisting, the Almighty! Were I to unveil to thine eyes the gates of this city, which have been fashioned by the right hand of might and power, thou wouldst behold that which none before thee hath ever beheld, and wouldst witness that which no other soul hath ever witnessed. Thou wouldst apprehend the most obscure signs and the most abstruse allusions, and wouldst clearly behold the mysteries of the beginning in the point of the end. All matters would be made easy unto thee, fire would be turned into light, knowledge and blessings, and thou wouldst abide in safety within the court of holiness.

Bereft, however, of the essence of the mysteries of His wisdom, which We have imparted unto thee beneath the veils of these blessed and soul-stirring words, thou wouldst fail to attain unto even a sprinkling of the oceans of divine knowledge or the crystal streams of divine power, and wouldst be recorded in the Mother Book, through the Pen of oneness and by the Finger of God, amongst the ignorant. Nor wouldst

1.18

1.19

thou be able to grasp a single word of the Book or a single utterance of the Kindred of God[12] concerning the mysteries of the beginning and the end.

1.20   O thou whom We have outwardly never met, yet whom We inwardly cherish in Our heart! Be fair in thy judgment and present thyself before Him Who seeth and knoweth thee, even if thou seest and knowest Him not: Can any soul be found to elucidate these words with such convincing arguments, clear testimonies, and unmistakable allusions as to appease the heart of the seeker and relieve the soul of the listener? Nay, by the One in Whose hand is My soul! Unto none is given to quaff even a dewdrop thereof unless he entereth within this city, a city whose foundations rest upon mountains of crimson-colored ruby, whose walls are hewn of the chrysolite of divine unity, whose gates are made of the diamonds of immortality, and whose earth sheddeth the fragrance of divine bounty.

1.21   Having imparted unto thee, beneath countless veils of concealment, certain hidden mysteries, We now return to Our elucidation of the Books of old, that perchance thy feet may not slip and thou mayest receive with complete certitude the portion which We shall bestow upon thee of the billowing oceans of life in the realm of the names and attributes of God.

1.22   It is recorded in all the Books of the Gospel that He Who is the Spirit* spoke in words of pure light unto His disciples, saying: "Know that heaven and earth may pass away, but my words shall never pass away."[13] As is clear and evident to

---

* Jesus.

thine eminence, these words outwardly mean that the Books of the Gospel will remain in the hands of people till the end of the world, that their laws shall not be abrogated, that their testimony shall not be abolished, and that all that hath been enjoined, prescribed, or ordained therein shall endure forever.

O My brother! Sanctify thy heart, illumine thy soul, 1.23 and sharpen thy sight, that thou mayest perceive the sweet accents of the Birds of Heaven and the melodies of the Doves of Holiness warbling in the Kingdom of eternity, and perchance apprehend the inner meaning of these utterances and their hidden mysteries. For otherwise, wert thou to interpret these words according to their outward meaning, thou couldst never prove the truth of the Cause of Him Who came after Jesus, nor silence the opponents, nor prevail over the contending disbelievers. For the Christian divines use this verse to prove that the Gospel shall never be abrogated and that, even if all the signs recorded in their Books were fulfilled and the Promised One appeared, He would have no recourse but to rule the people according to the ordinances of the Gospel. They contend that if He were to manifest all the signs indicated in the Books, but decree aught besides that which Jesus had decreed, they would neither acknowledge nor follow Him, so clear and self-evident is this matter in their sight.

Thou canst indeed hear the learned and the foolish 1.24 amongst the people voice the same objections in this day, saying: "The sun hath not risen from the West, nor hath the Crier cried out betwixt earth and heaven. Water hath not inundated certain lands; the Dajjál[14] hath not appeared; Súfyání[15] hath not arisen; nor hath the Temple been witnessed in the sun." I heard, with Mine own ears, one of their divines proclaim: "Should all these signs come to pass and the long-awaited Qá'im appear, and should He ordain, with respect to even our secondary laws, aught beyond that which hath been revealed in the Qur'án, we would assuredly charge Him with imposture, put Him to death, and refuse forever to acknowledge Him," and other statements such as these deniers make. And all this, when the Day of Resurrection hath been ushered in, and the Trumpet hath been sounded, and all the denizens of earth and heaven have been gathered together, and the Balance hath been appointed, and the Bridge hath been laid, and the Verses have been sent down, and the Sun hath shone forth, and the stars have been blotted out, and the souls have been raised to life, and the breath of the Spirit hath blown, and the angels have been arrayed in ranks, and Paradise hath been brought nigh, and Hell made to blaze! These things have all come to pass, and yet to this day not a single one of these people hath recognized them! They all lie as dead within their own shrouds, save those who have believed and repaired unto God, who rejoice in this day in His celestial paradise, and who tread the path of His good-pleasure.

1.25   Veiled as they remain within their own selves, the generality of the people have failed to perceive the sweet accents of holiness, inhale the fragrance of mercy, or seek guidance, as bidden by God, from those who are the custodians of the Scriptures. He proclaimeth, and His word, verily, is the truth: "Ask ye, therefore, of them that have the custody of the Scriptures, if ye know it not."[16] Nay rather, they have turned aside from them and followed instead the Sámirí[17] of their own idle fancies. Thus have they strayed far from the mercy of their Lord and failed to attain unto His Beauty in the day of His presence. For no sooner had He come unto them with a sign and a testimony from God than the same people who had eagerly awaited the day of His Revelation, who had called upon Him in the daytime and in the night season, who had implored Him to gather them together in His presence and to grant that they may lay down their lives in His path, be led aright by His guidance and illumined by His light—this very people condemned and reviled Him, and inflicted upon Him such cruelties as transcend both My capacity to tell and thine ability to hear them. My very pen crieth out at this moment and the ink weepeth sore and groaneth. By God! Wert thou to hearken with thine inner ear, thou wouldst in truth hear the lamentations of the denizens of heaven; and wert thou to remove the veil from before thine eyes, thou wouldst behold the Maids of Heaven overcome and the holy souls overwhelmed, beating upon their faces and fallen upon the dust.

Alas, alas, for that which befell Him Who was the Manifestation of the Self of God, and for that which He and His loved ones were made to suffer! The people inflicted upon them what no soul hath ever inflicted upon another, and what no infidel hath wrought against a believer or suffered at his hand. Alas, alas! That immortal Being sat upon the darksome dust, the Holy Spirit lamented in the retreats of glory, the pillars of the Throne crumbled in the exalted dominion, the joy of the world was changed into sorrow in the crimson land, and the voice of the Nightingale was silenced in the golden realm. Woe betide them for what their hands have wrought and for what they have committed! 1.26

Hearken then unto that which the Bird of Heaven uttered, in the sweetest and most wondrous accents, and in the most perfect and exalted melodies, concerning them— 1.27

an utterance that shall fill them with remorse from now unto "the day when mankind shall stand before the Lord of the worlds": "Although they had before prayed for victory over those who believed not, yet when there came unto them He of Whom they had knowledge, they disbelieved in Him. The curse of God on the infidels!"[18] Such indeed are their condition and attainments in their vain and empty life. Erelong shall they be cast into the fire of affliction and find none to help or succor them.

1.28   Be not veiled by aught that hath been revealed in the Qur'án, or by what thou hast learned from the works of those Suns of immaculacy and Moons of majesty,[19] regarding the perversion of the Texts by the fanatical or their alteration by their corruptors. By these statements only certain specific and clearly indicated passages are intended. In spite of My weakness and poverty, I would assuredly be able, should I so desire, to expound these passages unto thine eminence. But this would divert us from our purpose and lead us astray from the outstretched path. It would immerse us in limited allusions and distract us from that which is beloved in the court of the All-Praised.

1.29   O thou who art mentioned in this outspread roll and who, amidst the gloomy darkness that now prevaileth, hast been illumined by the splendors of the sacred Mount in the Sinai of divine Revelation! Cleanse thy heart from every blasphemous whispering and evil allusion thou hast heard in the past, that thou mayest inhale the sweet savors of eternity from the Joseph of faithfulness, gain admittance into the celestial Egypt, and perceive the fragrances of enlightenment from this resplendent and luminous Tablet, a Tablet wherein the Pen hath inscribed the ancient mysteries of the names of His Lord, the Exalted, the Most High. Perchance thou mayest be recorded in the holy Tablets among them that are well assured.

O thou who art standing before My Throne and yet remain unaware thereof! Know thou that whoso seeketh to scale the summits of the divine mysteries must needs strive to the utmost of his power and capacity for his Faith, that the pathway of guidance may be made clear unto him. And should he encounter One Who layeth claim to a Cause from God, and Who holdeth from His Lord a testimony beyond the power of men to produce, he must needs follow Him in all that He pleaseth to proclaim, command and ordain, even were He to decree the sea to be land, or to pronounce earth to be heaven, or that the former lieth above the latter or below it, or to ordain any change or transformation, for He, verily, is aware of the celestial mysteries, the unseen subtleties, and the ordinances of God. 1.30

Were the peoples of every nation to observe that which hath been mentioned, the matter would be made simple unto them, and such words and allusions would not withhold them from the Ocean of the names and attributes of God. And had the people known this truth, they would not have denied God's favors, nor would they have risen against, contended with, and rejected His Prophets. Similar passages are also to be found in the Qur'án, should the matter be carefully examined. 1.31

Know, moreover, that it is through such words that God proveth His servants and sifteth them, separating the believer from the infidel, the detached from the worldly, the pious from the profligate, the doer of good from the worker of iniquity, and so forth. Thus hath the Dove of holiness proclaimed: "Do men think when they say 'We believe' they shall be let alone and not be put to proof?"[20] 1.32

1.33   It behooveth him who is a wayfarer in the path of God and a wanderer in His way to detach himself from all who are in the heavens and on the earth. He must renounce all save God, that perchance the portals of mercy may be unlocked before his face and the breezes of providence may waft over him. And when he hath inscribed upon his soul that which We have vouchsafed unto him of the quintessence of inner meaning and explanation, he will fathom all the secrets of these allusions, and God shall bestow upon his heart a divine tranquility and cause him to be of them that are at peace with themselves. In like manner wilt thou comprehend the meaning of all the ambiguous verses that have been sent down concerning the question thou didst ask of this Servant Who abideth upon the seat of abasement, Who walketh upon the earth as an exile with none to befriend, comfort, aid, or assist Him, Who hath placed His whole trust in God, and Who proclaimeth at all times: "Verily we are God's, and to Him shall we return."[21]

1.34   Know thou that the passages that We have called "ambiguous" appear as such only in the eyes of them that have failed to soar above the horizon of guidance and to reach the heights of knowledge in the retreats of grace. For otherwise, unto them that have recognized the Repositories of divine Revelation and beheld through His inspiration the mysteries of divine authority, all the verses of God are perspicuous and all His allusions are clear. Such men discern the inner mysteries that have been clothed in the garment of words as clearly as ye perceive the heat of the sun or the wetness of water, nay even more distinctly. Immeasurably exalted is God above our praise of His loved ones, and beyond their praise of Him!

Now that We have reached this most excellent theme   1.35
and attained such lofty heights by virtue of that which hath
flowed from this Pen through the incomparable favors of
God, the Exalted, the Most High, it is Our wish to disclose
unto thee certain stations in the wayfarer's journey towards
his Creator. Perchance all that thine eminence hath desired
may be revealed unto thee, that the proof may be made
complete and the blessing abundant.

Know thou of a truth that the seeker must, at the beginning   1.36
of his quest for God, enter the Garden of Search. In this journey it behooveth the wayfarer to detach himself from all save
God and to close his eyes to all that is in the heavens and on
the earth. There must not linger in his heart either the hate or
the love of any soul, to the extent that they would hinder him
from attaining the habitation of the celestial Beauty. He must
sanctify his soul from the veils of glory and refrain from boast-
ing of such worldly vanities, outward knowledge, or other gifts
as God may have bestowed upon him. He must search after the
truth to the utmost of his ability and exertion, that God may
guide him in the paths of His favor and the ways of His mercy.
For He, verily, is the best of helpers unto His servants. He saith,
and He verily speaketh the truth: "Whoso maketh efforts for
Us, in Our ways shall We assuredly guide him."²² And further-
more: "Fear God and God will give you knowledge."²³

In this journey the seeker becometh witness to a myriad   1.37
changes and transformations, confluences and divergences.
He beholdeth the wonders of Divinity in the mysteries of
creation and discovereth the paths of guidance and the ways
of His Lord. Such is the station reached by them that search
after God, and such are the heights attained by those who
hasten unto Him.

1.38   When once the seeker hath ascended unto this station, he will enter the City of Love and Rapture, whereupon the winds of love will blow and the breezes of the spirit will waft. In this station the seeker is so overcome by the ecstasies of yearning and the fragrances of longing that he discerneth not his left from his right, nor doth he distinguish land from sea or desert from mountain. At every moment he burneth with the fire of longing and is consumed by the onslaught of separation in this world. He speedeth through the Paran of love and traverseth the Horeb of rapture. Now he laugheth, now he weepeth sore; now he reposeth in peace, now he trembleth in fear. Nothing can alarm him, naught can thwart his purpose, and no law can restrain him. He standeth ready to obey whatsoever His Lord should please to decree as to his beginning and his end. With every breath he layeth down his life and offereth up his soul. He bareth his breast to meet the darts of the enemy and raiseth his head to greet the sword of destiny; nay rather, he kisseth the hand of his would-be murderer and surrendereth his all. He yieldeth up spirit, soul, and body in the path of his Lord, and yet he doeth so by the leave of his Beloved and not of his own whim and desire. Thou findest him chill in the fire and dry in the sea, abiding in every land and treading every path. Whosoever toucheth him in this state will perceive the heat of his love. He walketh the heights of detachment and traverseth the vale of renunciation. His eyes are ever expectant to witness the wonders of God's mercy and eager to behold the splendors of His beauty. Blessed indeed are they that have attained unto such a station, for this is the station of the ardent lovers and the enraptured souls.

1.39   And when this stage of the journey is completed and the wayfarer hath soared beyond this lofty station, he entereth the City of Divine Unity, and the garden of oneness, and the court of detachment. In this plane the seeker casteth away all signs, allusions, veils, and words, and beholdeth all things with an eye illumined by the effulgent lights which God Himself hath shed upon him. In his journey he seeth all differences return to a single word and all allusions culminate in a single point. Unto this beareth witness he who sailed upon the ark of fire and followed the inmost path to the pinnacle of glory in the realm of immortality: "Knowledge is one point, which the foolish have multiplied."[24] This is the station that hath been alluded to in the tradition: "I am He, Himself, and He is I, Myself, except that I am that I am, and He is that He is."[25]

In this station, were He Who is the Embodiment of the End to say: "Verily, I am the Point of the Beginning," He would indeed be speaking the truth. And were He to say: "I am other than Him," this would be equally true. Likewise, were He to proclaim: "Verily, I am the Lord of heaven and earth," or "the King of kings," or "the Lord of the realm above," or Muḥammad, or ʿAlí, or their descendants, or aught else, He would indeed be proclaiming the truth of God. He, verily, ruleth over all created things and standeth supreme above all besides Him. Hast thou not heard what hath been said aforetime: "Muḥammad is our first, Muḥammad our last, Muḥammad our all"? And elsewhere: "They all proceed from the same Light"?

In this station the truth of the unity of God and of the signs of His sanctity is established. Thou shalt indeed see them all rising above the bosom of God's might and embraced in the arms of His mercy; nor can any distinction be made between His bosom and His arms. To speak of change or transformation in this plane would be sheer blas-

1.40

1.41

phemy and utter impiety, for this is the station wherein the light of divine unity shineth forth, and the truth of His oneness is expressed, and the splendors of the everlasting Morn are reflected in lofty and faithful mirrors. By God! Were I to reveal the full measure of that which He hath ordained for this station, the souls of men would depart from their bodies, the inner realities of all things would be shaken in their foundations, they that dwell within the realms of creation would be dumbfounded, and those who move in the lands of allusion would fade into utter nothingness.

1.42   Hast thou not heard: "No change is there in God's creation"?[26] Hast thou not read: "No change canst thou find in God's mode of dealing"?[27] Hast thou not borne witness to the truth: "No difference wilt thou see in the creation of the God of Mercy"?[28] Yea, by My Lord! They that dwell within this Ocean, they that ride upon this Ark, witness no change in the creation of God and behold no differences upon His earth. And if God's creation be not prone to change and alteration, how then could they who are the Manifestations of His own Being be subject to it? Immeasurably exalted is God above all that we may conceive of the Revealers of His Cause, and immensely glorified is He beyond all that they may mention in His regard!

1.43   Great God! This sea had laid up lustrous pearls in store;
        The wind hath raised a wave that casteth them ashore.
        So put away thy robe and drown thyself therein,
        And cease to boast of skill: it serveth thee no more!

1.44   If thou be of the inmates of this city within the ocean of divine unity, thou wilt view all the Prophets and Messengers of God as one soul and one body, as one light and one spirit, in such wise that the first among them would be last and the last would be first. For they have all arisen to proclaim His Cause and have established the laws of divine wisdom. They are, one and all, the Manifestations of His Self, the Repositories of His might, the Treasuries of His Revelation, the Dawning-Places of His splendor, and the Daysprings of His light. Through them are manifested the signs of sanctity in the realities of all things and the tokens of oneness in the essences of all beings. Through them are revealed the elements of glorification in the heavenly realities and the exponents of praise in the eternal essences. From them hath all creation proceeded and unto them shall return all that hath been mentioned. And since in their inmost Beings they are the same Luminaries and the self-same Mysteries, thou shouldst view their outward conditions in the same light, that thou mayest recognize them all as one Being, nay, find them united in their words, speech, and utterance.

Wert thou to consider in this station the last of them to be the first, or conversely, thou wouldst indeed be speaking the truth, as hath been ordained by Him Who is the Wellspring of Divinity and the Source of Lordship: "Say: Call upon God or call upon the All-Merciful: by whichsoever name ye will, invoke him, for He hath most excellent names."[29] For they are all the Manifestations of the name of God, the Dawning-Places of His attributes, the Repositories of His might, and the Focal Points of His sovereignty, whilst God—magnified be His might and glory—is in His Essence sanctified above all names and exalted beyond even the loftiest attributes. Consider likewise the evidences of divine omnipotence both in their Souls and in their human 1.45

Temples, that thine heart may be assured and that thou mayest be of them that speed through the realms of His nearness.

1.46   I shall restate here My theme, that perchance this may assist thee in recognizing thy Creator. Know thou that God—exalted and glorified be He—doth in no wise manifest His inmost Essence and Reality. From time immemorial He hath been veiled in the eternity of His Essence and concealed in the infinitude of His own Being. And when He purposed to manifest His beauty in the kingdom of names and to reveal His glory in the realm of attributes, He brought forth His Prophets from the invisible plane to the visible, that His name "the Manifest" might be distinguished from "the Hidden" and His name "the Last" might be discerned from "the First," and that there may be fulfilled the words: "He is the First and the Last; the Seen and the Hidden; and He knoweth all things!"[30] Thus hath He revealed these most excellent names and most exalted words in the Manifestations of His Self and the Mirrors of His Being.

1.47   It is therefore established that all names and attributes return unto these sublime and sanctified Luminaries. Indeed, all names are to be found in their names, and all attributes can be seen in their attributes. Viewed in this light, if thou wert to call them by all the names of God, this would be true, as all these names are one and the same as their own Being. Comprehend then the intent of these words, and guard it within the tabernacle of thy heart, that thou mayest recognize the implications of thine inquiry, fulfill them according to that which God hath ordained for thee, and thus be numbered with those who have attained unto His purpose.

All that thou hast heard regarding Muḥammad the son   1.48
of Ḥasan[31]—may the souls of all that are immersed in the
oceans of the spirit be offered up for His sake—is true beyond
the shadow of a doubt, and we all verily bear allegiance unto
Him. But the imáms of the Faith have fixed His abode in
the city of Jábulqá,[32] which they have depicted in strange
and marvelous signs. To interpret this city according to the
literal meaning of the tradition would indeed prove impossible, nor can such a city ever be found. Wert thou to search
the uttermost corners of the earth, nay probe its length and
breadth for as long as God's eternity hath lasted and His
sovereignty will endure, thou wouldst never find a city such
as they have described, for the entirety of the earth could
neither contain nor encompass it. If thou wouldst lead Me
unto this city, I could assuredly lead thee unto this holy
Being, Whom the people have conceived according to what
they possess and not to that which pertaineth unto Him!
Since this is not in thy power, thou hast no recourse but to
interpret symbolically the accounts and traditions that have
been reported from these luminous souls. And, as such an
interpretation is needed for the traditions pertaining to the
aforementioned city, so too is it required for this holy Being.
When thou hast understood this interpretation, thou shalt
no longer stand in need of "transformation" or aught else.

Know then that, inasmuch as all the Prophets are but   1.49
one and the same soul, spirit, name, and attribute, thou
must likewise see them all as bearing the name Muḥammad
and as being the son of Ḥasan, as having appeared from the
Jábulqá of God's power and from the Jábulṣá of His mercy.
For by Jábulqá is meant none other than the treasure-houses
of eternity in the all-highest heaven and the cities of the

unseen in the supernal realm. We bear witness that Muḥam-mad, the son of Ḥasan, was indeed in Jábulqá and appeared therefrom. Likewise, He Whom God shall make manifest abideth in that city until such time as God will have estab-lished Him upon the seat of His sovereignty. We, verily, acknowledge this truth and bear allegiance unto each and every one of them. We have chosen here to be brief in our elucidation of the meanings of Jábulqá, but if thou be of them that truly believe, thou shalt indeed comprehend all the true meanings of the mysteries enshrined within these Tablets.

1.50 But as to Him Who appeared in the year sixty, He stan-deth in need of neither transformation nor interpretation, for His name was Muḥammad, and He was a descendent of the Imáms of the Faith. Thus it can be truly said of Him that He was the son of Ḥasan, as is undoubtedly clear and evident unto thine eminence. Nay, He it is Who fashioned that name and created it for Himself, were ye to observe with the eye of God.

1.51 It is Our wish at this juncture to digress from Our theme to recount that which befell the Point of the Qur'án,* and to extol His remembrance, that perchance thou mayest gain into all things an insight born of Him Who is the Almighty, the Incomparable.

1.52 Consider and reflect upon His days, when God raised Him up to promote His Cause and to stand as the repre-sentative of His own Self. Witness how He was assailed, denied, and denounced by all; how, when He set foot in the streets and marketplaces, the people derided Him, wagged

---

* Muḥammad.

their heads at Him, and laughed Him to scorn; how at every moment they sought to slay Him. Such were their doings that the earth in all its vastness was straitened for Him, the Concourse on High bewailed His plight, the foundations of existence were reduced to nothingness, and the eyes of the well-favored denizens of His Kingdom wept sore over Him. Indeed, so grievous were the afflictions which the infidels and the wicked showered upon Him that no faithful soul can bear to hear them.

If these wayward souls had indeed paused to reflect upon their conduct, recognized the sweet melodies of that Mystic Dove singing upon the twigs of this snow-white Tree, embraced that which God had revealed unto and bestowed upon them, and discovered the fruits of the Tree of God upon its branches, wherefore then did they reject and denounce Him? Had they not lifted their heads to the heavens to implore His appearance? Had they not besought God at every moment to honor them with His Beauty and sustain them through His presence?

1.53

But as they failed to recognize the accents of God and the divine mysteries and holy allusions enshrined in that which flowed from the tongue of Muḥammad, and as they neglected to examine the matter in their own hearts, and followed instead those priests of error who have hindered the progress of the people in past dispensations and who will continue to do so in future cycles, they were thus veiled from the divine purpose, failed to quaff from the celestial streams, and deprived themselves of the presence of God, the Manifestation of His Essence, and the Dayspring of His eternity. Thus did they wander in the paths of delusion and the ways of heedlessness, and return to their abode in that fire which

1.54

feedeth on their own souls. These, verily, are numbered with the infidels whose names have been inscribed by the Pen of God in His holy Book. Nor have they ever found, or will ever find, a friend or helper.

1.55 Had these souls but clung steadfastly to the Handle of God manifested in the Person of Muḥammad, had they turned wholly unto God and cast aside all that they had learned from their divines, He would assuredly have guided them through His grace and acquainted them with the sacred truths that are enshrined within His imperishable utterances. For far be it from His greatness and His glory that He should turn away a seeker at His door, cast aside from His Threshold one who hath set his hopes on Him, reject one who hath sought the shelter of His shade, deprive one who hath held fast to the hem of His mercy, or condemn to remoteness the poor one who hath found the river of His riches. But as these people failed to turn wholly unto God, and to hold fast to the hem of His all-pervading mercy at the appearance of the Daystar of Truth, they passed out from under the shadow of guidance and entered the city of error. Thus did they become corrupt and corrupt the people. Thus did they err and lead the people into error. And thus were they recorded among the oppressors in the books of heaven.

1.56 Now that this evanescent One hath reached this exalted point in the exposition of the inner mysteries, the reason for the denial of these uncouth souls will be described briefly, that it may serve as a testimony unto them that are endued with understanding and insight, and be a token of My favor unto the concourse of the faithful.

1.57 Know then that when Muḥammad, the Point of the Qur'án and the Light of the All-Glorious, came with perspicuous verses and luminous proofs manifested in such signs as are beyond the power of all existence to produce, He bade all men follow this lofty and outstretched Path in accordance with the precepts that He had brought from God. Whoso acknowledged Him, recognized the signs of God in His inmost Being, and saw in His beauty the changeless beauty of God, the decree of "resurrection," "ingathering," "life," and "paradise" was passed upon him. For he who had believed in God and in the Manifestation of His beauty was raised from the grave of heedlessness, gathered together in the sacred ground of the heart, quickened to the life of faith and certitude, and admitted into the paradise of the divine presence. What paradise can be loftier than this, what ingathering mightier, and what resurrection greater? Indeed, should a soul be acquainted with these mysteries, he would grasp that which none other hath fathomed.

Know then that the paradise that appeareth in the day   1.58 of God surpasseth every other paradise and excelleth the realities of Heaven. For when God—blessed and glorified is He—sealed the station of prophethood in the person of Him Who was His Friend, His Chosen One, and His Treasure amongst His creatures, as hath been revealed from the Kingdom of glory: "but He is the Apostle of God and the Seal of the Prophets,"[33] He promised all men that they shall attain unto His own presence in the Day of Resurrection. In this He meant to emphasize the greatness of the Revelation to come, as it hath indeed been manifested through the power of truth. And there is of a certainty no paradise greater than this, nor station higher, should ye reflect upon the verses of the Qur'án. Blessed be he who knoweth of a certainty that he shall attain unto the presence of God on that day when His Beauty shall be made manifest.

1.59　　Were I to recount all the verses that have been revealed in connection with this exalted theme, it would weary the reader and divert Us from Our purpose. The following verse shall therefore suffice Us; may thine eyes be solaced therewith, and mayest thou attain unto that which hath been treasured and concealed therein: "It is God who hath reared the heavens without pillars thou canst behold; then mounted His throne, and imposed laws on the sun and moon: each traveleth to its appointed goal. He ordereth all things. He maketh His signs clear, that ye may have firm faith in the presence of your Lord."[34]

1.60　　Ponder then, O My friend, the words "firm faith" that have been mentioned in this verse. It saith that the heavens and the earth, the throne, the sun and the moon, all have been created to the end that His servants may have unswerving faith in His presence in His days. By the righteousness of God! Contemplate, O My brother, the greatness of this station, and behold the condition of the people in these days, fleeing from the Countenance of God and His Beauty "as though they were affrighted asses."[35] Wert thou to reflect upon that which We have revealed unto thee, thou wouldst undoubtedly grasp Our purpose in this utterance and discover that which We have desired to impart unto thee within this paradise. Perchance thine eyes may rejoice in beholding it, thine ears take delight in hearing that which is recited therein, thy soul be enthralled by recognizing it, thy heart illumined by comprehending it, and thy spirit gladdened by the fragrant breezes that waft therefrom. Haply thou mayest attain unto the pinnacle of divine grace and abide within the Riḍván of transcendent holiness.

He, however, who denied God in His Truth, who turned   1.61
his back upon Him and rebelled, who disbelieved and made
mischief, the verdict of "impiety," "blasphemy," "death,"
and "fire" was passed upon him. For, what blasphemy is
greater than to turn unto the manifestations of Satan, to
follow the doctors of oblivion and the people of rebellion?
What impiety is more grievous than to deny the Lord on the
day when faith itself is renewed and regenerated by God,
the Almighty, the Beneficent? What death is more wretched
than to flee from the Source of everlasting life? What fire
is fiercer on the Day of Reckoning than that of remoteness
from the divine Beauty and the celestial Glory?

These were the very words and utterances used by the   1.62
pagan Arabs living in the days of Muḥammad to dispute
with and pronounce judgment against Him. They said:
"Those who believed in Muḥammad dwelt in our midst
and associated with us day and night. When did they die
and when were they raised again to life?" Hearken unto that
which was revealed in reply: "If ever thou dost marvel, marvelous surely is their saying, 'What! When we have become
dust and moldering bones, shall we be restored in a new creation?'"[36] And in another passage: "And if thou shouldst say,
'After death ye shall surely be raised again,' the infidels will
certainly exclaim, 'This is naught but palpable sorcery.'"[37]
Thus did they mock and deride Him, for they had read in
their Books and heard from their divines the terms "life"
and "death," and understood them as this elemental life and
physical death, and hence when they found not that which
their vain imaginings and their false and wicked minds
had conceived, they hoisted the banners of discord and the

standards of sedition and kindled the flame of war. God, however, quenched it through the power of His might, as thou seest again in this day with these infidels and evil-doers.

1.63   At this hour, when the sweet savors of attraction have wafted over Me from the everlasting city, when transports of yearning have seized Me from the land of splendors at the dawning of the Daystar of the worlds above the horizon of 'Iráq, and the sweet melodies of Ḥijáz have brought to Mine ears the mysteries of separation, I have purposed to relate unto thine eminence a portion of that which the Mystic Dove hath warbled in the midmost heart of Paradise as to the true meaning of life and death, though the task be impossible. For were I to interpret these words for thee as it hath been inscribed in the Guarded Tablets, all the books and pages of the world could not contain it, nor could the souls of men bear its weight. I shall nonetheless mention that which beseemeth this day and age, that it might serve as a guidance unto whosoever desireth to gain admittance into the retreats of glory in the realms above, to hearken unto the melodies of the spirit intoned by this divine and mystic bird, and to be numbered with those who have severed themselves from all save God and who in this day rejoice in the presence of their Lord.

1.64   Know then that "life" hath a twofold meaning. The first pertaineth to the appearance of man in an elemental body, and is as manifest to thine eminence and to others as the midday sun. This life cometh to an end with physical death, which is a God-ordained and inescapable reality. That life, however, which is mentioned in the Books of the Prophets and the Chosen Ones of God is the life of knowledge; that is to say, the servant's recognition of the sign of the splendors wherewith He Who is the Source of all splendor hath Himself invested him, and his certitude of attaining unto the presence of God through the Manifestations of His Cause. This is that blessed and everlasting life that perisheth not: whosoever is quickened thereby shall never die, but will endure as long as His Lord and Creator will endure.

The first life, which pertaineth to the elemental body, 1.65 will come to an end, as hath been revealed by God: "Every soul shall taste of death."[38] But the second life, which ariseth from the knowledge of God, knoweth no death, as hath been revealed aforetime: "Him will We surely quicken to a blessed life."[39] And in another passage concerning the martyrs: "Nay, they are alive and sustained by their Lord."[40] And from the Traditions: "He who is a true believer liveth both in this world and in the world to come."[41] Numerous examples of similar words are to be found in the Books of God and of the Embodiments of His justice. For the sake of brevity, however, We have contented Ourself with the above passages.

O My brother! Forsake thine own desires, turn thy face 1.66 unto thy Lord, and walk not in the footsteps of those who have taken their corrupt inclinations for their god, that perchance thou mayest find shelter in the heart of existence, beneath the redeeming shadow of Him Who traineth all names and attributes. For they who turn away from their Lord in this day are in truth accounted amongst the dead, though to outward seeming they may walk upon the earth, amongst the deaf, though they may hear, and amongst the blind, though they may see, as hath been clearly stated by Him Who is the Lord of the Day of Reckoning: "Hearts have they with which they understand not, and eyes have they with which they see not. . . ."[42] They walk the edge of a treacherous bank and tread the brink of a fiery abyss.[43] They partake not of the billows of this surging and treasure-laden Ocean, but disport themselves with their own idle words.

1.67   In this connection We will relate unto thee that which was revealed of old concerning "life," that perchance it may turn thee away from the promptings of self, deliver thee from the narrow confines of thy prison in this gloomy plane, and aid thee to become of them that are guided aright in the darkness of this world.

1.68   He saith, and He, verily, speaketh the truth: "Shall the dead whom We have quickened, and for whom We have ordained a light whereby he may walk amongst men, be like him whose likeness is in the darkness, whence he will not come forth?"[44] This verse was revealed with respect to Ḥamzih and Abú-Jahl, the former of whom was a believer whilst the latter disbelieved. Most of the pagan leaders mocked and derided it, were agitated, and clamored: "How did Ḥamzih die? And how was he restored to his former life?" Were ye to examine carefully the verses of God, ye would find many such statements recorded in the Book.

1.69   Would that pure and stainless hearts could be found, that I might impart unto them a sprinkling from the oceans of knowledge which My Lord hath bestowed upon Me, so that they may soar in the heavens even as they walk upon the earth and speed over the waters even as they course the land, and that they may take up their souls in their hands and lay them down in the path of their Creator. Howbeit, leave hath not been granted to divulge this mighty secret. Indeed, it hath been from everlasting a mystery enshrined within the treasuries of His power and a secret concealed within the repositories of His might, lest His faithful servants forsake their own lives in the hope of attaining this most great station in the realms of eternity. Nor shall they who wander in this oppressive darkness ever attain unto it.

O My brother! At every juncture We have restated Our theme, that all that hath been recorded in these verses may, by the leave of God, be made clear unto thee, and that thou mayest become independent of those who are plunged in the darkness of self and who tread the valley of arrogance and pride, and be of them that move within the paradise of everlasting life. 1.70

Say: O people! The Tree of Life hath verily been planted in the heart of the heavenly paradise and bestoweth life in every direction. How can ye fail to perceive and recognize it? It will in truth aid thee to grasp all that this well-assured Soul hath disclosed unto thee of the essence of the divine mysteries. The Dove of holiness warbleth in the heaven of immortality and admonisheth thee to array thyself with a new vesture, wrought of steel to shield thee from the shafts of doubt concealed in the allusions of men, saying: "Except a man be born of water and of the Spirit, he cannot enter into the kingdom of God. That which is born of the flesh is flesh; and that which is born of the Spirit is spirit. Marvel not that I said unto thee, ye must be born again."45 1.71

Wing then thy flight unto this divine Tree and partake of its fruits. Gather up that which hath fallen therefrom and guard it faithfully. Meditate then upon the utterance of one of the Prophets as He intimated to the souls of men, through veiled allusions and hidden symbols, the glad-tidings of the One Who was to come after Him, that thou mayest know of 1.72

a certainty that their words are inscrutable to all save those who are endued with an understanding heart. He saith: "His eyes were as a flame of fire," and "brass-like were His feet," and "out of His mouth goeth a two-edged sword."[46] How could these words be literally interpreted? Were anyone to appear with all these signs, he would assuredly not be human. And how could any soul seek his company? Nay, should he appear in one city, even the inhabitants of the next would flee from him, nor would any soul dare approach him! Yet, shouldst thou reflect upon these statements, thou wouldst find them to be of such surpassing eloquence and clarity as to mark the loftiest heights of utterance and the epitome of wisdom. Methinks it is from them that the suns of eloquence have appeared and the stars of clarity have dawned forth and shone resplendent.

1.73 Behold, then, the foolish ones of bygone times and those who, in this day, await the advent of such a being! Nor would they ever bear allegiance unto him except that he appear in the aforementioned form. And as such a being will never appear, so too will they never believe. Such indeed is the measure of the understanding of these perverse and ungodly souls! How could those who fail to understand the most evident of the evident and the most manifest of the manifest ever apprehend the abstruse realities of the divine precepts and the essence of the mysteries of His everlasting wisdom?

1.74 I shall now briefly explain the true meaning of this utterance, that thou mayest discover its hidden mysteries and be of them that perceive. Examine then and judge aright that which We shall reveal unto thee, that haply thou mayest be accounted in the sight of God amongst those who are fair-minded in these matters.

Know then that He who uttered these words in the realms 1.75
of glory meant to describe the attributes of the One Who is
to come in such veiled and enigmatic terms as to elude the
understanding of the people of error. Now, when He saith:
"His eyes were as a flame of fire," He alludeth but to the
keenness of sight and acuteness of vision of the Promised
One, Who with His eyes burneth away every veil and cover-
ing, maketh known the eternal mysteries in the contingent
world, and distinguisheth the faces that are obscured with
the dust of hell from those that shine with the light of paradise.[47] Were His eyes not made of the blazing fire of God,
how could He consume every veil and burn away all that
the people possess? How could He behold the signs of God
in the Kingdom of His names and in the world of creation?
How could He see all things with the all-perceiving eye
of God? Thus have we conferred upon Him a penetrating
vision in this day. Would that ye believe in the verses of God!
For, indeed, what fire is fiercer than this flame that shineth
in the Sinai of His eyes, whereby He consumeth all that
hath veiled the peoples of the world? Immeasurably exalted
shall God remain above all that hath been revealed in His
unerring Tablets concerning the mysteries of the beginning
and the end until that day when the Crier will cry out, the
day whereon we shall all return unto Him.

As to the words "brass-like were His feet," by this is meant 1.76
His constancy upon hearing the call of God that comman-
deth Him: "Be thou steadfast as thou hast been bidden."[48]
He shall so persevere in the Cause of God, and evince such

firmness in the path of His might, that even if all the powers of earth and heaven were to deny Him, He would not waver in the proclamation of His Cause, nor flee from His command in the promulgation of His Laws. Nay rather, He will stand as firm as the highest mountains and the loftiest peaks. He will remain immovable in His obedience to God and steadfast in revealing His Cause and proclaiming His Word. No obstacle will hinder Him, nor will the censure of the froward deter Him or the repudiation of the infidels cause Him to waver. All the hatred, the rejection, the iniquity, and the unbelief that He witnesseth serve but to strengthen His love for God, to augment the yearning of His heart, to heighten the exultation of His soul, and to fill His breast with passionate devotion. Hast thou ever seen in this world brass stronger, or blade sharper, or mountain more unyielding than this? He shall verily stand upon His feet to confront all the inhabitants of the earth, and will fear no one, notwithstanding that which, as thou well knowest, the people are wont to commit. Glory be to God, Who hath established Him and called Him forth! Potent is God to do what He pleaseth. He, in truth, is the Help in Peril, the Self-Subsisting.

1.77   And further He saith: "Out of his mouth goeth a two-edged sword." Know thou that since the sword is an instrument that divideth and cleaveth asunder, and since there proceedeth from the mouth of the Prophets and the Chosen Ones of God that which separateth the believer from the infidel and the lover from the beloved, this term hath been so employed, and apart from this dividing and separating no other meaning is intended. Thus, when He Who is the

Primal Point* and the eternal Sun desireth, by the leave of God, to gather together all creation, to raise them up from the graves of their own selves, and to divide them one from another, He shall pronounce but one verse from Him, and this verse will distinguish truth from error from this day unto the Day of Resurrection. What sword is sharper than this heavenly sword, what blade more trenchant than this incorruptible steel that severeth every tie and separateth thereby the believer from the infidel, father from son, brother from sister, and lover from beloved?⁴⁹ For whoso believeth in that which hath been revealed unto him is a true believer and whoso turneth away is an infidel, and such an irrevocable separation occurreth between them that they will cease to consort and associate with each other in this world. And so it is between father and son, for should the son believe and the father deny, they will be severed and forever dissociated from each other. Nay rather, thou witnesseth how the son slayeth the father and the father the son. Consider in the same light all that We have explained and related unto thee.

Wert thou to behold all things with the eye of discernment, thou wouldst indeed see that this divine sword doth cleave asunder generations. Would that ye could understand it! All this is by virtue of the word of separation that is manifested on the Day of Judgment and Separation, were the people to take heed in the days of their Lord. Nay, couldst thou but sharpen thy sight and refine thy heart, thou wouldst witness that all the material swords which in every day and age have slain the infidels and waged war against the impious proceed

1.78

---

* The Báb.

from this divine and invisible sword. Open then thine eyes, that thou mayest behold all that We have revealed to thee and attain unto that which none other hath attained. We verily exclaim: "Praise be to God, He Who is the Lord of the Day of Reckoning!"[50]

1.79   Yea, inasmuch as these people have failed to acquire true knowledge from its source and wellspring, and from the ocean of fresh and soft-flowing waters that stream, by the leave of God, through hearts that are pure and stainless, they have been veiled from that which God hath intended by those words and allusions and have remained confined within the prison of their own selves.

1.80   We render thanks unto God for that which He hath bestowed upon us of His grace. He it is Who hath caused us to be assured of the truth of His Faith—a Faith which the combined forces of earth and heaven are powerless to resist. He it is Who hath enabled us to acknowledge Him in the day of His presence, to testify unto Him Whom God shall make manifest in the latter Resurrection, and to be among them that have believed in Him ere His appearance, that His favor may be made complete unto us and unto all mankind.

1.81   But hear, O My brother, My plaint against them that claim to be associated with God and with the Manifestations of His knowledge, and yet follow their corrupt inclinations, consume the substance of their neighbor, are given to wine, commit murder, defraud and slander each other, hurl calumnies against God, and are wont to speak falsely. The people attribute all these deeds unto Us, whilst their perpetrators remain shameless before God. They cast aside that which He hath enjoined upon them and commit that which He hath forbidden. Yet it behooveth the people of truth that the signs of humility should shine upon their faces, that the light of sanctity should radiate from their countenances, that they should walk upon the earth as though they were in the presence of God and distinguish themselves in their deeds from all the dwellers of the earth. Such must be their state that their eyes should behold the evidences of His might, their tongues and hearts make mention of His name, their feet be set towards the lands of His nearness, and their hands take fast hold upon His precepts. And were they to pass through a valley of pure gold and mines of precious silver, they should regard them as wholly unworthy of their attention.

These people, however, have turned aside from all this and placed instead their affections upon that which accordeth with their own corrupt inclinations. Thus do they roam in the wilderness of arrogance and pride. I bear witness at this moment that God is wholly quit of them, and likewise are We. We beseech God to suffer Us not to associate with them either in this life or in the life to come. He, verily, is the Eternal Truth. No God is there but Him, and His might is equal to all things. 1.82

Quaff then, O My brother, from the living waters that We have caused to flow in the oceans of these words. Methinks the seas of grandeur are surging within them, and the gems of divine virtue are shining within and upon them. Divest then thyself of that which debarreth thee from this fathomless crimson sea, and to the cry of "In the name of God and by His grace!" immerse thyself therein. Let the fear of no one dismay thee. Trust in the Lord, thy God, for He is sufficient unto whosoever trusteth in Him. He, verily, shall protect thee, and in Him shalt thou abide in safety. 1.83

1.84   Know thou, moreover, that in this most hallowed and resplendent city thou shalt find the wayfarer to be lowly before all men and humble before all things. For naught doth he behold save that he perceiveth God therein. He beholdeth the effulgent glories of God in the lights of His Revelation that have encompassed the Sinai of creation. In this station the wayfarer must not claim the seat of honor in any gathering or walk before others in the desire to vaunt and exalt himself. Rather must he regard himself as standing at all times in the presence of his Lord. He must not wish for anyone that which he doth not wish for himself, nor speak that which he would not bear to hear spoken by another, nor yet desire for any soul that which he would not have desired for himself. It befitteth him, rather, to walk upon the earth with undeviating steps in the kingdom of His new creation.

1.85   Know, however, that the seeker, at the outset of his journey, witnesseth change and transformation, as hath already been mentioned. This is undoubtedly the truth, as hath been revealed concerning those days: "On the day when the earth shall be changed into another earth."[51] These are indeed days the like of which no mortal eye hath ever seen. Blessed is he that attaineth thereunto and realizeth their full worth. "We had sent Moses with Our signs, saying unto him: 'Bring forth thy people from darkness into light and remind them of the days of God.'"[52] And these are in truth the days of God, could ye but know it.

1.86   In this station, all changing and varying realities are manifest before thee. Whosoever denieth this truth hath verily turned aside from the Cause of God, rebelled against His rule, and gainsaid His sovereignty. For it is indeed within the power of Him Who changeth the earth into another earth to transform all that dwell and move thereon. Wherefore marvel not at how He turneth darkness into light, light into darkness, ignorance into knowledge, error into guidance, death into life, and life into death. It is in this station that the law of transformation taketh effect. Ponder thereon, if thou be of them that tread this path, that all thou didst ask of this lowly One may be made plain unto thee and that thou mayest abide within the tabernacle of this guidance. For He doeth whatsoever He willeth and ordaineth whatsoever He pleaseth. Nor shall He be asked of His doings, whilst all men will be asked of their every deed.[53]

O My brother! In this stage, which marketh the beginning of the journey, thou shalt behold divers stations and differing signs, even as was mentioned in connection with the City of Search. All these hold true in their respective planes. It behooveth thine eminence in this station to consider each created thing in its own place, neither abasing nor exalting its true rank. For instance, if thou wert to reduce the unseen world to the realm of creation, this would be an act of sheer blasphemy, and the converse would likewise be the essence of impiety. Wert thou, however, to describe the unseen world and the realm of creation within their own stations, this would be the undoubted truth. In other words, wert thou to witness any transformation in the realm of the divine unity, no greater sin could be conceived in all creation, but wert thou to consider transformation in its own place and understand it accordingly, no harm could befall thee. 1.87

By My Lord! Notwithstanding all that We have revealed unto thee of the mysteries of utterance and the degrees of exposition, methinks I have spoken not a single letter of 1.88

the ocean of God's hidden knowledge and the essence of His inscrutable wisdom. God willing, this We shall erelong accomplish in its appointed time. He verily, remembereth all things in their own place, and we, in truth, all yield praise unto Him.

1.89   Know thou, moreover, that the bird that taketh flight in the atmosphere of the realm on high will never be able to soar unto the heaven of transcendent holiness, nor taste of the fruits which God hath brought forth therein, nor quaff from the streams which He hath caused to flow in its midst. And were it to partake but a drop thereof, it would perish forthwith. Even as thou dost witness in these days with regard to those who profess allegiance unto Us, and yet perform such deeds, utter such words, and advance such claims as they have. Methinks they lie as dead within their own veils.

1.90   Comprehend, in like manner, every station, sign, and allusion, that thou mayest perceive all things in their own place and consider all matters in their proper light. For in this station, the City of Divine Unity, are to be found those who have entered within the ark of divine guidance and journeyed through the heights of divine unity. Thou shalt behold the lights of beauty upon their faces and the mysteries of glory in their human temples. Thou shalt perceive the musk-laden fragrance of their words and behold the signs of His sovereignty in all their ways and doings. Nor wilt thou be veiled by the deeds of them that have failed to quaff from the crystal springs or to attain unto the cities of holiness, and who follow their selfish desires and spread disorder in the land, all the while believing themselves to be guided aright. It is indeed of them that it hath been said: "These are the abject and foolish, who follow every clamorous impostor and who bend with every changing wind."[54] The stages of this journey, station, and abode are clear and manifest to thee and require no further explanation.

Know then that all thou hast heard and witnessed that Daystar of Truth, the Primal Point, ascribe to Himself from the designations of former times is only on account of the weakness of men and the scheme of the world of creation. Otherwise, all names and attributes revolve round His Essence and circle about the threshold of His sanctuary. For He it is Who traineth all names, revealeth all attributes, conferreth life upon all beings, proclaimeth the divine verses, and arrayeth the heavenly signs. Nay, shouldst thou gaze with thine inner eye, thou wouldst find that all save Him fade into utter nothingness and are as a thing forgotten in His holy presence. "God was alone; there was none else besides Him. He remaineth now what He hath ever been." Since it hath been established that God—hallowed and glorified be He!—was alone and there was none besides Him, how can the law of change and transformation apply here? Shouldst thou reflect upon that which We have disclosed unto thee, the daystar of guidance would shine resplendent before thee in this everlasting morn, and thou wouldst be numbered therein with the pious. 1.91

Know, moreover, that all that We have mentioned concerning these journeys is intended for none but the elect amongst the righteous. And shouldst thou spur on the charger of the spirit and traverse the meads of heaven, thou wouldst complete all these journeys and discover every mystery in less than the twinkling of an eye. 1.92

O My brother! If thou be a champion of this arena, speed within the lands of certitude, that thy soul may be delivered in this day from the bondage of misbelief, and that thou 1.93

mayest perceive the sweet savors that waft from this garden. Verily, the perfume-laden breezes that carry the fragrance of this city blow over all regions. Forfeit not thy portion thereof and be not of the heedless. How well hath it been said:

1.94   His fragrant breaths diffused in Eastern lands could well
To sick ones in the West restore their sense of smell![55]

1.95   After this heavenly journey and mystical ascent the wayfarer will enter within the Garden of Wonderment. Were I to disclose unto thee the reality of this station, thou wouldst lament and bewail the plight of this Servant Who remaineth in the hands of these infidels, Who hath grown perplexed at His plight, and is lost in bewilderment in this fathomless ocean. They conspire each day to put Me to death, and seek at every hour to banish Me from this land, even as they banished Me from another land. Yet this Servant standeth ready before them, awaiting whatsoever the Almighty hath ordained and decreed for Us. Nor do I fear any soul, encompassed as We may be by such trials and tribulations as are inflicted by the wicked and the malicious and surrounded at this hour by a myriad woes and sorrows. "Noah's flood is but the measure of the tears I have shed, and Abraham's fire an ebullition of My soul. Jacob's grief is but a reflection of My sorrows, and Job's afflictions a fraction of My calamity."[56]

1.96   Were I to recount unto thine eminence the dire adversities that have befallen Me, thou wouldst be so grieved as to forsake the mention of all things and to forget thyself and all that the Lord hath created on earth. But as this is not Our wish, I have concealed the revelation of the divine decree in the heart of Bahá and veiled it from the eyes of all that move in the realm of creation, that it may lie hid within the tabernacle of the Unseen until such time as God will have revealed its secret. "Naught in the heavens or on the earth can escape His knowledge, and He, verily, perceiveth all things."[57]

As We have digressed from Our theme, let Us leave aside 1.97 these allusions and return to Our discussion of this city. Verily, whoso entereth therein shall be saved, and whoso turneth aside therefrom will assuredly perish.

O thou who art mentioned in these Tablets! Know thou 1.98 that he who embarketh upon this journey will marvel at the signs of the power of God and the wondrous evidences of His handiwork. Bewilderment will seize him from every side, even as hath been attested by that Essence of immortality from the Concourse on high: "Increase My wonder and amazement at Thee, O God!"[58] Well hath it been said:

I knew not what amazement was 1.99
    Until I made Thy love my cause.
O how amazing would it be
    If I were not amazed by Thee![59]

In this valley the wayfarers stray and perish ere they attain 1.100 their final abode. Gracious God! So immense is this valley, so vast this city in the kingdom of creation, that it seemeth to have neither beginning nor end. How great the blessedness of him who completeth his journey therein and who traverseth, through the assistance of God, the hallowed soil of this heavenly city, a city in which the favored ones of God and the pure in heart are overcome with wonder and awe. And We say: "Praise be to God, the Lord of the worlds."

And should the servant ascend to even loftier heights, 1.101 quit this mortal world of dust, and seek to ascend unto the celestial abode, he will then pass from this city into the City of Absolute Nothingness, that is, of dying to self and living in God. In this station, this most exalted habitation, this journey of utter self-effacement, the wayfarer forgetteth his soul, spirit, body, and very being, immerseth himself in the sea of nothingness, and liveth on earth as one unworthy of mention. Nor will one find any sign of his existence, for he hath vanished from the realm of the visible and attained unto the heights of self-abnegation.

1.102   Were We to recount the mysteries of this city, the dominions of the hearts of men would be laid to waste in the intensity of their longing for this mighty station. For this is the station wherein the effulgent glories of the Beloved are revealed to the sincere lover and the resplendent lights of the Friend are cast upon the severed heart that is devoted to Him.

1.103   How can a true lover continue to exist when once the effulgent glories of the Beloved are revealed? How can the shadow endure when once the sun hath shone forth? How can a devoted heart have any being before the existence of the Object of its devotion? Nay, by the One in Whose hand is my soul! In this station, the seeker's complete surrender and utter effacement before his Creator will be such that, were he to search the East and the West, and traverse land, sea, mountain and plain, he would find no trace of his own self or of any other soul.

1.104   Gracious God! But for fear of the Nimrod of tyranny and for the protection of the Abraham of justice, I would reveal unto thee that which, wert thou to abandon self and desire, would enable thee to dispense with aught else and to draw nigh unto this city. Be patient, however, until such time as

God will have proclaimed His Cause. He, verily, rewardeth beyond measure them that endure with patience.[60] Inhale then the sweet savors of the spirit from the garment of hidden meanings, and say: "O ye that are immersed in the ocean of selflessness! Hasten to enter the City of Immortality, if ye seek to ascend its heights." And We exclaim: "Verily we are God's, and to Him shall we return."[61]

From this most august and exalted station, and from this most sublime and glorious plane, the seeker entereth the City of Immortality, therein to abide forever. In this station he beholdeth himself established upon the throne of independence and the seat of exaltation. Then will he comprehend the meaning of that which hath been revealed of old concerning the day "whereon God shall enrich all through His abundance."[62] Well is it with them that have attained unto this station and drunk their fill from this snow-white chalice before this Crimson Pillar. 1.105

Having, in this journey, immersed himself in the ocean of immortality, rid his heart from attachment to aught save Him, and attained unto the loftiest heights of everlasting life, the seeker will see no annihilation either for himself or for any other soul. He will quaff from the cup of immortality, tread in its land, soar in its atmosphere, consort with them that are its embodiments, partake of the imperishable and incorruptible fruits of the tree of eternity, and be forever accounted, in the lofty heights of immortality, amongst the denizens of the everlasting realm. 1.106

All that existeth in this city shall indeed endure and will never perish. Shouldst thou, by the leave of God, enter this sublime and exalted garden, thou wouldst find its sun in its noontide glory, never to set, never to be eclipsed. The 1.107

same holdeth true of its moon, its firmament, its stars, trees, and oceans, and of all that pertaineth thereunto or existeth therein. By Him besides Whom there is none other God! Were I to recount, from this day unto the end that hath no end, its wondrous attributes, the love that My heart cherisheth for this hallowed and everlasting city would never be exhausted. I shall, however, bring My theme to a close, since time is short and the inquirer impatient, and since these secrets are not to be openly divulged save by the leave of God, the Almighty, the All-Compelling.

1.108   Erelong shall the faithful behold, in the day of the latter Resurrection, Him Whom God shall make manifest descending with this city from the heaven of the Unseen, together with a company of His exalted and favored angels. Great, therefore, is the blessedness of him that attaineth unto His presence and beholdeth His countenance. We all, verily, cherish this hope, and exclaim: "Praise be unto Him, for verily He is the Eternal Truth, and unto Him do we return!"

1.109   Know, moreover, that should one who hath attained unto these stations and embarked upon these journeys fall prey to pride and vainglory, he would at that very moment come to naught and return to the first step without realizing it. Indeed, they that seek and yearn after Him in these journeys are known by this sign, that they humbly defer to those who have believed in God and in His verses, that they are lowly before those who have drawn nigh unto Him and unto the Manifestations of His Beauty, and that they bow in submission to them that are firmly established upon the lofty heights of the Cause of God and before its majesty.

1.110   For were they to reach the ultimate object of their quest for God and their attainment unto Him, they would have but reached that abode which hath been raised up within their own hearts. How then could they ever hope to ascend unto such realms as have not been ordained for them or created for their station? Nay, though they journey from everlasting to everlasting, they will never attain unto Him Who is the midmost Heart of existence and the Axis of the entire creation, He on Whose right hand flow the seas of grandeur, on Whose left stream the rivers of might, and Whose court none can ever hope to reach, how much less His very abode! For He dwelleth in the ark of fire, speedeth, in the sphere of fire, through the ocean of fire, and moveth within the atmosphere of fire. How can he who hath been fashioned of contrary elements ever enter or even approach this fire? Were he to do so, he would be instantly consumed.

Know, moreover, that should the cord of assistance binding this mighty Pivot to the dwellers of earth and heaven be severed, they would all assuredly perish. Great God! How can the lowly dust ever reach unto Him Who is the Lord of lords? Immeasurably exalted is God above that which they conceive in their hearts, and immensely glorified is He beyond that which they attribute to Him. 1.111

Yea, the seeker reacheth a station wherein that which hath been ordained for him knoweth no bounds. The fire of love so blazeth in his heart that it seizeth the reins of constraint from his grasp. At every moment his love for his Lord increaseth and draweth him nearer unto his Creator, in such wise that if his Lord be in the east of nearness, and he dwell in the west of remoteness and possess all that earth and heaven contain of rubies and gold, he would forsake it all and rush forth to the land of the Desired One. And shouldst thou find him to be otherwise, know assuredly that 1.112

such a man is a lying impostor. We, verily, all belong unto Him Whom God shall make manifest in the latter Resurrection, and through Him shall we be raised again to life.

1.113   In these days, inasmuch as We have lifted not the veils that conceal the countenance of the Cause of God, nor disclosed unto men the fruits of these stations which We have been forbidden to describe, thou beholdest them drunk with heedlessness. Otherwise, were the glory of this station to be revealed unto men to an extent smaller than a needle's eye, thou wouldst witness them gathering before the threshold of divine mercy and hastening from all sides to the court of nearness in the realms of divine glory. We have concealed it, however, as mentioned before, that those who believe may be distinguished from them that deny, and that those who turn unto God may be discerned from them that turn aside. I verily proclaim: "There is no power nor strength except in God, the Help in Peril, the Self-Subsisting."

1.114   From this station the wayfarer ascendeth unto a City that hath no name or description, and whereof one heareth neither sound nor mention. Therein flow the oceans of eternity, whilst this city itself revolveth round the seat of eternity. Therein the sun of the Unseen shineth resplendent above the horizon of the Unseen, a sun that hath its own heavens and its own moons, which partake of its light and which rise from and set upon the ocean of the Unseen. Nor can I ever hope to impart even a dewdrop of that which hath been decreed therein, as none is acquainted with its mysteries save God, its Creator and Fashioner, and His Manifestations.

1.115   Know, moreover, that when We undertook to reveal these words and committed some of them to writing, it was Our intention to elucidate for thine eminence, in the sweet accents of the blessed and the well-favored of God, all that We had previously mentioned of the words of the Prophets and the sayings of the Messengers. Time, however, was lacking, and the traveler who came from thy presence was in great haste and eager to return. Thus have We cut short Our discourse and contented Ourself with this much, without completing the description of these stages in a seemly and befitting manner. Indeed, We have omitted the description of major cities and mighty journeys. Such was the haste of the courier that We even forsook the mention of the two exalted journeys of Resignation and Contentment.

Yet, should thine eminence reflect upon these brief statements, thou wouldst assuredly acquire every knowledge, attain unto the Object of all learning, and exclaim: "Sufficient are these words unto all creation both visible and invisible!" 1.116

Even so, should the fire of love burn within thy soul, thou wouldst ask: "Is there yet any more?"[63] And We say: "Praise be to God, the Lord of the worlds!" 1.117

2

TABLET TO MÁNIKCHÍ ṢÁḤIB (LAWḤ-I-MÁNIKCHÍ-ṢÁḤIB)

IN THE NAME OF
THE ONE TRUE GOD

Praise be to the all-perceiving, the ever-abiding Lord Who, 2.1
from a dewdrop out of the ocean of His grace, hath reared
the firmament of existence, adorned it with the stars of knowledge, and admitted man into the lofty court of insight and
understanding. This dewdrop, which is the Primal Word of
God, is at times called the Water of Life, inasmuch as it quick-
eneth with the waters of knowledge them that have perished
in the wilderness of ignorance. Again it is called the Primal
Light, a light born of the Sun of divine knowledge, through
whose effulgence the first stirrings of existence were made
plain and manifest. Such manifestations are the expressions of
the grace of Him Who is the Peerless, the All-Wise. He it is
who knoweth and bestoweth all. He it is who transcendeth all
that hath been said or heard. His knowledge will remain forever above the grasp of human vision and understanding and
beyond the reach of human words and deeds. To the truth
of this utterance existence itself and all that hath appeared
therefrom bear eloquent testimony.

It is clear and evident, therefore, that the first bestowal 2.2
of God is the Word, and its discoverer and recipient is the
power of understanding. This Word is the foremost instruc-

tor in the school of existence and the revealer of Him Who is the Almighty. All that is seen is visible only through the light of its wisdom. All that is manifest is but a token of its knowledge. All names are but its name, and the beginning and end of all matters must needs depend upon it.

2.3   Thy letter hath reached this captive of the world in His prison.[1] It brought joy, strengthened the ties of friendship, and renewed the memory of bygone days. Praise be to the Lord of creation Who granted us the favor of meeting in the Arabian land,* wherein we visited and held converse. It is Our hope that our encounter may never be forgotten nor effaced from the heart by the passage of time, but rather that, out of the seeds thus sown, the sweet herbs of friendship may spring forth and remain forever fresh and verdant for all to behold.

2.4   As to thy question concerning the heavenly Scriptures: The All-Knowing Physician hath His finger on the pulse of mankind. He perceiveth the disease, and prescribeth, in His unerring wisdom, the remedy. Every age hath its own problem, and every soul its particular aspiration. The remedy the world needeth in its present-day afflictions can never be the same as that which a subsequent age may require. Be anxiously concerned with the needs of the age ye live in, and center your deliberations on its exigencies and requirements.

2.5   We can well perceive how the whole human race is encompassed with great, with incalculable afflictions. We see it languishing on its bed of sickness, sore-tried and disillusioned. They that are intoxicated by self-conceit have interposed themselves between it and the Divine and infallible Physician. Wit-

---

* 'Iráq

ness how they have entangled all men, themselves included, in the mesh of their devices. They can neither discover the cause of the disease, nor have they any knowledge of the remedy. They have conceived the straight to be crooked, and have imagined their friend an enemy.

Incline your ears to the sweet melody of this Prisoner. 2.6 Arise, and lift up your voices, that haply they that are fast asleep may be awakened. Say: O ye who are as dead! The Hand of Divine bounty proffereth unto you the Water of Life. Hasten and drink your fill. Whoso hath been reborn in this Day, shall never die; whoso remaineth dead, shall never live.

Thou hast written concerning languages. Both Arabic and 2.7 Persian are laudable. That which is desired of a language is that it convey the intent of the speaker, and either language can serve this purpose. And since in this Day the Orb of divine knowledge hath risen in the firmament of Persia, that tongue deserveth every praise.

O friend! When the Primal Word appeared amongst men 2.8 in these latter days, a number of heavenly souls recognized the voice of the Beloved and bore allegiance unto it, whilst others, finding the deeds of some to be at variance with their words, remained far removed from the spreading rays of the Sun of divine knowledge.

Say: O children of dust! He Who is the Spirit of Purity 2.9 saith: In this glorious Day whatsoever can purge you from defilement and ensure your peace and tranquility, that indeed is the Straight Path,² the path that leadeth unto Me. To be purged from defilement is to be cleansed of that which is injurious to man and detracteth from his high station— among which is to take undue pleasure in one's own words and deeds, notwithstanding their unworthiness. True peace and tranquility will only be realized when every soul will have become the well-wisher of all mankind. He Who is the All-Knowing beareth Me witness: were the peoples of the world to grasp the true significance of the words of God, they would never be deprived of their portion of the ocean of His bounty. In the firmament of truth there hath never been, nor will there ever be, a brighter star than this.

2.10   The first utterance of Him Who is the All-Wise is this: O children of dust! Turn your faces from the darkness of estrangement to the effulgent light of the daystar of unity. This is that which above all else will benefit the peoples of the earth. O friend! Upon the tree of utterance there hath never been, nor shall there ever be, a fairer leaf, and beneath the ocean of knowledge no pearl more wondrous can ever be found.

2.11   O children of understanding! If the eyelid, however delicate, can deprive man's outer eye from beholding the world and all that is therein, consider then what would be wrought if the veil of covetousness were to descend upon his inner eye. Say: O people! The darkness of greed and envy becloudeth the radiance of the soul even as the clouds obstruct the light of the sun. Should anyone hearken unto this utterance with a discerning ear, he will unfurl the wings of detachment and soar effortlessly in the atmosphere of true understanding.

2.12   At a time when darkness had encompassed the world, the ocean of divine favor surged and His Light was made manifest, that the doings of men might be laid bare. This, verily, is that Light which hath been foretold in the heavenly scriptures. Should the Almighty so please, the hearts of all men will be purged and purified through His goodly utterance, and the light of unity will shed its radiance upon every soul and revive the whole earth.

O people! Words must be supported by deeds, for deeds are the true test of words. Without the former, the latter can never quench the thirst of the yearning soul, nor unlock the portals of vision before the eyes of the blind. The Lord of celestial wisdom saith: A harsh word is even as a sword thrust; a gentle word as milk. The latter leadeth the children of men unto knowledge and conferreth upon them true distinction. 2.13

The Tongue of Wisdom proclaimeth: He that hath Me not is bereft of all things. Turn ye away from all that is on earth and seek none else but Me. I am the Sun of Wisdom and the Ocean of Knowledge. I cheer the faint and revive the dead. I am the guiding Light that illumineth the way. I am the royal Falcon on the arm of the Almighty. I unfold the drooping wings of every broken bird and start it on its flight.[3] 2.14

The incomparable Friend saith: The path to freedom hath been outstretched; hasten ye thereunto. The wellspring of wisdom is overflowing; quaff ye therefrom. Say: O well-beloved ones! The tabernacle of unity hath been raised; regard ye not one another as strangers. Ye are the fruits of one tree, and the leaves of one branch. Verily I say, whatsoever leadeth to the decline of ignorance and the increase of knowledge hath been, and will ever remain, approved in the sight of the Lord of creation. Say: O people! Walk ye neath the shadow of justice and truthfulness and seek ye shelter within the tabernacle of unity. 2.15

2.16 Say: O ye that have eyes to see! The past is the mirror of the future. Gaze ye therein and be apprised thereof; perchance ye may be aided thereby to recognize the Friend and may be not the cause of His displeasure. In this Day the choicest fruit of the tree of knowledge is that which serveth the welfare of humanity and safeguardeth its interests.

2.17 Say: The tongue hath been created to bear witness to My truth; defile it not with falsehood. The heart is the treasury of My mystery; surrender it not into the hand of covetous desires. We fain would hope that in this resplendent morn, when the effulgent rays of the Sun of divine knowledge have enveloped the whole earth, we may all attain unto the good pleasure of the Friend and drink our fill from the ocean of His recognition.

2.18 O friend! As hearing ears are scarce to find, the pen hath for some time remained silent in its quarters. In truth, matters have come to such a pass that silence hath taken precedence over utterance and hath come to be regarded as preferable. Say: O people! These words are being uttered in due measure, that the newly born may thrive and the tender shoot flourish. Milk should be given in suitable proportion, that the children of the world may attain to the station of maturity and abide in the court of oneness.

2.19 O friend! We came upon a pure soil and sowed therein the seeds of true understanding. Let it now be seen what the rays of the sun will do—whether they will cause these seeds to wither or to grow. Say: Through the ascendancy of God, the All-Knowing, the Incomparable, the Luminary of divine understanding hath, in this Day, risen from behind the veil of the spirit, and the birds of every meadow are intoxicated with the wine of knowledge and exhilarated with the remembrance of the Friend. Well is it with them that discover and hasten unto Him!

3
RESPONSES TO QUESTIONS OF MÁNIK<u>CH</u>Í ṢÁḤIB FROM A TABLET TO MÍRZÁ ABU'L-FAḌL

In regard to what thou hast written concerning his honor   3.1
the learned Ṣáḥib, upon him be the grace of God, his state
of mind and disposition are clear and evident, as is further
attested by that which he hath sent. Now, as to his questions, it was not deemed advisable to refer and reply to each
one individually, for the response would have run counter
to wisdom and been incompatible with that which is current amongst men. Even so, in that which was revealed in
his honor from the heaven of divine favor, answers were
provided in a language of marvelous concision and clarity.
But it appeareth that he hath failed to consider the matter
closely, for otherwise he would have readily admitted that
not a single point was omitted, and would have exclaimed:
"This is naught but a clear and conclusive utterance!" His
questions were the following.

First: "The Prophets of Mahábád, together with Zoro-   3.2
aster, were twenty-eight in number. Each one of them sought
to exalt, rather than abrogate, the faith and religion of the
others. Each one that appeared bore witness to the truth and
veracity of the former law and religion and breathed no word
about abolishing them. Each declared: 'We are the bearers of
a revelation from God, which We deliver unto His servants.'
Some of the Hindu Prophets, however, have declared: 'We
are God Himself, and it is incumbent upon the entire cre-

ation to bear allegiance unto Us. Whensoever conflict and dissension appear amongst men, We arise to quench it.' Each one that appeared announced: 'I am the same One that appeared in the beginning.' The latter Prophets such as David, Abraham, Moses and Jesus confirmed the truth of the Prophets gone before them, but said: 'Such was the law in the past, but in this day the law is that which I proclaim.' The Arabian Prophet,* however, hath said: 'Through My appearance every law hath proven to be unsound and no law holdeth but Mine.' Which of these creeds is acceptable and which of these leaders is to be preferred?"

3.3   It should first be noted that in one sense the stations of the Prophets of God differ one from another. For instance, consider Moses. He brought forth a Book and established ordinances, whilst a number of the Prophets and Messengers who arose after Him were charged with the promulgation of His laws, insofar as they remained consonant with the needs of the age. The books and chronicles annexed to the Torah bear eloquent testimony to this truth.

3.4   Regarding the statement ascribed to the Author of the Qur'án: "Through My appearance every law and religion hath proven to be unsound and no law holdeth but Mine," no such words were ever uttered by that Source and Fount of divine wisdom. Nay rather, He confirmed that which had been sent down before from the empyrean of the Divine Will unto the Prophets and Messengers of God. He saith, exalted be His utterance: "Alif. Lám. Mím. God! There is no God but Him, the Living, the Ever-Abiding. He it is Who hath

---

* Muḥammad

70

sent down to Thee the Book through the power of truth, confirming those which preceded it. He revealed aforetime the Torah and the Evangel as a guidance unto men, and He hath now revealed the Qur'án. . . ."[1] He, moreover, hath asserted that all the Prophets have proceeded from God and have returned unto Him. Viewed in this light, they are all as one and the same Being, inasmuch as they have not uttered a word, brought a message, or revealed a cause, of their own accord. Nay, all that they have said hath proceeded from the one true God, exalted be His glory. They have all summoned men unto the Supreme Horizon and imparted the tidings of eternal life. Thus the diverse statements recounted by his honor the Ṣáḥib are to be seen as concordant letters, that is, letters that form a single word.

Concerning the question: "Which of these creeds is acceptable and which of these leaders is to be preferred?" this is the station wherein the following blessed words shine resplendent as the sun: "No distinction do We make between any of the Messengers,"[2] while the verse "Some of the Apostles We have caused to excel the others"[3] pertaineth to the other station of which We have already made mention. Indeed, the answer to all that his honor the Ṣáḥib hath asked lieth enshrined within this all-embracing, this weighty and incomparable utterance, hallowed and exalted be His word: "As to thy question concerning the heavenly Scriptures: The All-Knowing Physician hath His finger on the pulse of mankind. He perceiveth the disease, and prescribeth, in His unerring wisdom, the remedy. Every age hath its own problem, and every soul its particular aspiration. The remedy the world needeth in its present-day afflictions can never be the same as that which a subsequent age may

3.5

require. Be anxiously concerned with the needs of the age ye live in, and center your deliberations on its exigencies and requirements."[4] Every fair-minded soul will testify that these words are to be viewed as a mirror of the knowledge of God, wherein all that hath been inquired is clearly and conspicuously reflected. Blessed is he who hath been endowed with seeing eyes by God, the All-Knowing, the All-Wise.

3.6 Another question raised by the distinguished Ṣáḥib is the following: "There are four schools of thought in the world. One school affirmeth that all the visible worlds, from atoms to suns, constitute God Himself and that naught can be seen but Him. Another school claimeth that God is that Essence that must of necessity exist, that His Messengers are the intermediaries between Him and His creatures, and that their mission is to lead humanity unto Him. Yet another school holdeth that the stars were created by the Necessary Being,[5] whilst all other things are their effect and outcome. These things continually appear and disappear, even as the minute creatures that are generated in a pool of water. A further school maintaineth that the Necessary Being hath fashioned Nature through whose effect and agency all things, from atoms to suns, appear and disappear without beginning or end. What need then for an account or reckoning? As the grass groweth with the coming of the rain and vanisheth thereafter, so it is with all things. If the Prophets and the kings have instituted laws and ordinances, the proponents of this school argue, this hath merely been for the sake of preserving the civil order and regulating human society. The Prophets and the kings, however, have acted in different ways: the former have said 'God hath spoken thus' that the people might submit and obey, whilst the latter have resorted to the sword and the cannon. Which of these four schools is approved in the sight of God?"

Answer: The answer to all this falleth under the purview of the first utterance that hath streamed forth from the tongue of the All-Merciful. By God! It embraceth and comprehendeth all that hath been mentioned. He saith: "Be anxiously concerned with the needs of the age ye live in, and center your deliberations on its exigencies and requirements." For in this day He Who is the Lord of Revelation hath appeared and He Who spoke on Sinai is calling aloud. Whatsoever He may ordain is the surest foundation for the mansions reared in the cities of human knowledge and wisdom. Whoso holdeth fast unto it will be reckoned in the eyes of the Almighty among them that are endued with insight.

3.7

These sublime words have streamed forth from the Pen of the Most High. He saith, exalted be His glory: "This is the day of vision, for the countenance of God is shining resplendent above the horizon of Manifestation. This is the day of hearing, for the call of God hath been raised. It behooveth everyone in this day to uphold and proclaim that which hath been revealed by Him Who is the Author of all scripture, the Dayspring of revelation, the Fount of knowledge and the Source of divine wisdom." It is thus clear and evident that the reply to his question hath been revealed in the kingdom of utterance by Him Who is the Exponent of the knowledge of the All-Merciful. Happy are they that understand!

3.8

As to the four schools mentioned above, it is clear and evident that the second standeth closer to righteousness.[6] For the Apostles and Messengers of God have ever been the channels of His abounding grace, and whatsoever man hath

3.9

received from God hath been through the intermediary of those Embodiments of holiness and Essences of detachment, those Repositories of His knowledge and Exponents of His Cause. One can, however, provide a justification for the tenets of the other schools, for in a sense all things have ever been and shall ever remain the manifestations of the names and attributes of God.

3.10 As to the Ṣáḥib's reference to the kings, they are indeed the manifestations of the name of God "the Almighty" and the revealers of His name "the All-Powerful." The vesture that beseemeth their glorious temples is justice. Should they become adorned therewith, mankind will partake of perfect tranquility and infinite blessings.

3.11 Whoso hath quaffed of the wine of divine knowledge will indeed be able to answer such questions with clear and perspicuous proofs from the world without and with manifest and luminous evidences from the world within. A different Cause, however, hath appeared in this day and a different discourse is required. Indeed, with the inception of the year nine the time for questions and answers came to an end. Thus He, hallowed and magnified be His name, saith: "This is not the day for any man to question his Lord. When thou hearest the call of God voiced by Him Who is the Dayspring of grandeur, cry out: 'Here am I, O Lord of all names! Here am I, O Maker of the heavens! I testify that Thou hast revealed Thyself and hast revealed whatsoever Thou didst desire at Thine Own behest. Thou, in truth, art the Lord of strength and might.'"

3.12 The answer to all that the distinguished Ṣáḥib hath asked is clear and evident. The intent of that which was sent down in his honor from the heaven of divine providence was that he might give ear to the wondrous melodies of the Dove of Eternity and the gentle murmuring of the inhabitants of the most exalted Paradise, and that he might perceive the sweetness of the call and set foot upon the path.

One day the Tongue of Glory uttered a word in regard to 3.13
the Ṣáhib indicating that he may erelong be aided to perform a deed that would immortalize his name. When his letter was received in His holy and exalted Court, He said: "O Servant in attendance! Although his honor Mánikchí hath written only to ask concerning the sayings of others, yet from His letter We inhale the sweet savors of affection. Beseech the one true God to graciously aid him to do His will and pleasure. His might, in truth, is equal to all things." From this utterance of the All-Merciful there wafteth a fragrant breath. He, verily, is the All-Knowing, the All-Informed.

Another inquiry made by him is the following: "The 3.14
laws of Islám are based on religious principles and jurisprudence,[7] but in the Mahábád and Hindu religions there are only principles, and all laws, even those regarding the drinking of water or giving and taking in marriage, are considered a part of these principles, as are all other matters of human life. Kindly indicate which view is acceptable in the sight of God, exalted be His mention."

Religious principles have various degrees and stations. The 3.15
root of all principles and the cornerstone of all foundations hath ever been, and shall remain, the recognition of God. And these days are indeed the vernal season of the recognition of the All-Merciful. Whatsoever proceedeth in this day from the Repository of His Cause and the Manifestation of His Self is, in truth, the fundamental principle unto which all must bear allegiance.

3.16   The answer to this question is also embodied in these
blessed, these weighty and exalted words: "Be anxiously
concerned with the needs of the age ye live in, and center your deliberations on its exigencies and requirements."
For this day is the Lord of all days, and whatsoever hath
been revealed therein by the Source of divine Revelation is
the truth and the essence of all principles. This day may
be likened to a sea and all other days to gulfs and channels
that have branched therefrom. That which is uttered and
revealed in this day is the foundation, and is accounted as
the Mother Book and the Source of all utterance. Although
every day is associated with God, magnified be His glory,
yet these days have been singled out and adorned with the
ornament of intimate association with Him, for they have
been extolled in the books of the Chosen Ones of God, as
well as of some of His Prophets, as the "Day of God." In
a sense this day and that which appeareth therein are to be
regarded as the primary principles, while all other days and
whatsoever appeareth in them are to be viewed as the secondary ordinances deduced therefrom, and which as such are
subordinate and relative. For instance, attending the mosque
is secondary with respect to the recognition of God, for the
former is dependent upon and conditioned by the latter. As
to the principles current amongst the divines of this age,
these are merely a set of rules which they have devised and
from which they infer, each according to his own opinions
and inclinations, the ordinances of God.

3.17   Consider for example the question of immediate com-
pliance or postponement. God, exalted be His glory, saith:
"Eat and drink. . . ."[8] Now, it is not known whether this
ordinance must be complied with immediately or if its exe-

cution may be justifiably postponed. Some believe that it may be decided by external circumstances. Once one of the distinguished divines of Najaf set out to visit the Shrine of Imám Ḥusayn, peace be upon Him, accompanied by a number of his pupils. In the course of their journey they were waylaid by a group of Bedouin. The aforementioned divine immediately handed over all his possessions. Whereupon his pupils exclaimed: "Your eminence hath always favored postponement in such matters. What prompteth you now to act with such haste?" Pointing to the spears of the Bedouin, he replied: "The force of external circumstances, my friends!"

The founder of the principles of Islámic jurisprudence 3.18 was Abú-Ḥanífih, who was a prominent leader of the Sunnis. Such principles had existed in former times as well, as hath already been mentioned. In this day, however, the approval or rejection of all things dependeth wholly upon the Word of God. These differences are not worthy of mention. The eye of divine mercy casteth its glance upon all that is past. It behooveth us to mention them only in favorable terms, for they do not contradict that which is essential. This servant testifieth to his ignorance and beareth witness that all knowledge is with God, the Help in Peril, the Self-Subsisting.

Whatsoever runneth counter to the Teachings in this day 3.19 is condemned, for the Sun of Truth is shining resplendent above the horizon of knowledge. Happy are they who, with the waters of divine utterance, have cleansed their hearts from all allusions, whisperings and suggestions, and who have fixed their gaze upon the Dayspring of Glory. This, indeed, is the most gracious favor and the purest bounty. Whosoever hath attained thereunto hath attained unto all good, for otherwise the knowledge of aught else but God hath never proven, nor shall it ever prove, profitable unto men.

3.20   That which was mentioned in connection with religious principles and secondary ordinances referreth to the pronouncements which the divines of various religions have made, each according to his own capacity. At present, however, it behooveth us to follow His injunction to "leave them to their vain disputes."⁹ He, verily, speaketh the truth and leadeth the way. The decree is God's, the Almighty, the All-Bounteous.

3.21   Another of his questions: "Some maintain that whatsoever is in accordance with the dictates of nature and of the intellect must needs be both permissible and compulsory in the divine law, and conversely that one should refrain from observing that which is incompatible with these standards. Others believe that whatsoever hath been enjoined by the divine law and its blessed Author should be accepted without rational proof or natural evidence and obeyed without question or reservation, such as the march between Safa and Marwah, the stoning of the pillar of Jamrah,¹⁰ the washing of one's feet during ablutions, and so on. Kindly indicate which of these positions is acceptable."

3.22   Intellect hath various degrees. As a discussion of the pronouncements made by the philosophers in this connection would pass beyond the scope of our discourse, we have refrained from mentioning them. It is nonetheless indisputably clear and evident that the minds of men have never been, nor shall they ever be, of equal capacity. The Perfect Intellect alone can provide true guidance and direction. Thus were these sublime words revealed by the Pen of the Most High, exalted be His glory, in response to this question: "The Tongue of Wisdom proclaimeth: He that hath Me not is bereft of all things. Turn ye away from all that is on earth and seek none else but Me. I am the Sun of Wisdom and the Ocean of Knowledge. I cheer the faint and revive the dead. I am the guiding Light that illumineth the way. I am the royal Falcon on the arm of the Almighty. I unfold the drooping wings of every broken bird and start it on its flight."[11]

Consider how clearly the answer hath been revealed from the heaven of divine knowledge. Blessed are those who ponder it, who reflect upon it, and who apprehend its meaning! By the Intellect mentioned above is meant the universal divine Mind. How often hath it been observed that certain human minds, far from being a source of guidance, have become as fetters upon the feet of the wayfarers and prevented them from treading the straight path! The lesser intellect being thus circumscribed, one must search after Him Who is the ultimate Source of knowledge and strive to recognize Him. And should one come to acknowledge that Source round Whom every mind doth revolve, then whatsoever He should ordain is the expression of the dictates of a consummate wisdom. His very Being, even as the sun, is distinct from all else beside Him. The whole duty of man is to recognize Him; once this hath been achieved, then whatsoever He may please to ordain is binding and in full accordance with the requirements of divine wisdom. Thus have ordinances and prohibitions of every kind been laid down by the Prophets of the past, even unto the earliest times. 3.23

Certain deeds that are undertaken in this day are intended to emblazon the name of God, and the Pen of the Most 3.24

High hath fixed a recompense for those who perform them. Indeed, should any soul breathe but a fleeting breath for the sake of God, his recompense will become manifest, as attested by this mighty verse which was sent down from the empyrean of the divine Will to the Lord of Mecca,* blessed and glorified be He: "We did not appoint that which Thou wouldst have to be the Qiblih, but that We might know him who followeth the Apostle from him who turneth on his heels."[12]

3.25   Were anyone to meditate upon this blessed and transcendent Revelation and to ponder the verses that have been sent down, he would readily bear witness that the one true God is immeasurably exalted above His creatures, and that the knowledge of all things hath ever been and shall ever remain with Him. Every fair-minded soul, moreover, will testify that whosoever faileth to embrace the truth of this most great Revelation will find himself powerless and incapable of establishing the validity of any other cause or creed. And as to those who have deprived themselves of the robe of justice and arisen to promote the cause of iniquity, they shall give voice to that which the exponents of hatred and fanaticism have uttered from time immemorial. The knowledge of all things is with God, the All-Knowing, the All-Informed.

3.26   One day when this servant was in His presence, I was asked: "O servant in attendance! Wherewith art thou engaged?" "I am penning a reply," I answered, "to his honor Mírzá Abu'l-Faḍl." I was bidden: "Write to Mírzá Abu'l-Faḍl, may My glory be upon him, and say: 'Matters have

---

* Muḥammad

come to such a pass that the people of the world have grown accustomed to iniquity and flee from fair-mindedness. A divine Manifestation Who hath extolled and magnified the one true God, exalted be His glory, Who hath borne witness to His knowledge and confessed that His Essence is sanctified above all things and exalted beyond every comparison—such a Manifestation hath been called at various times a worshipper of the sun or a fire-worshipper. How numerous are those sublime Manifestations and Revealers of the Divine of Whose stations the people remain wholly unaware, of Whose grace they are utterly deprived, nay, God forbid, Whom they curse and revile!

"'One of the great Prophets Whom the foolish ones of 3.27 Persia in this day reject uttered these sublime words: "The sun is but a dense and spherical mass. It deserveth not to be called God or the Almighty. For the almighty Lord is He Whom no human comprehension can ever conceive, Whom no earthly knowledge can circumscribe, and Whose Essence none hath ever been or shall ever be able to fathom." Consider how eloquently, how solemnly He hath affirmed the very truth that God is proclaiming in this day. And yet He is not even deemed a believer by these abject and foolish ones, let alone seen as possessed of a sublime station! In another connection He said: "All existence hath appeared from His existence, and were it not for God, no creature would have ever existed and been attired with the raiment of being." May the Lord shield us all from the wickedness of such as have disputed the truth of God and of His loved ones and turned away from that Dayspring whereunto all the Books of God, the Help in Peril, the Self-Subsisting, have testified.'"

3.28   From that which hath been mentioned, it is clear that not every intellect can be the criterion of truth. The truly wise are, in the first place, the Chosen Ones of God, magnified be His glory—they Whom He hath singled out to be the Treasuries of His knowledge, the Repositories of His Revelation, the Daysprings of His authority and the Dawning-places of His wisdom, they Whom He hath made His representatives on earth and through Whom He revealeth that which He hath purposed. Whoso turneth unto them hath turned unto God, and whoso turneth away shall not be remembered in the presence of God, the All-Knowing, the All-Wise.

3.29   The universal criterion is that which hath just been mentioned. Whosoever attaineth thereunto, that is, who recognizeth and acknowledgeth the Dawning-place of God's Revelation, will be recorded in the Book of God among them that are endued with understanding. Otherwise he is naught but an ignorant soul, though he believe himself to be possessed of every wisdom. Now, were a person to see himself standing in the presence of God, were he to sanctify his soul from earthly attachments and evil intentions, and reflect upon that which hath been revealed in this most great Revelation from its inception to this day, he would readily testify that every detached soul, every perfect mind, sanctified being, attentive ear, penetrating eye, eloquent tongue, and joyous and radiant heart circleth round and boweth down, nay prostrateth itself in submission, before the mighty throne of God.

3.30   Another of his questions is this: "Among the Manifestations of the past one hath, in His time, allowed the eating of beef while another hath forbidden it; one hath permitted the eating of pork whereas another hath proscribed it. Thus do their ordinances differ. I entreat the True One, exalted be His name, to graciously specify the appropriate religious prohibitions."

A direct reply and detailed explanation of this matter would have overstepped the bounds of wisdom, inasmuch as people of diverse faiths associate with the distinguished Ṣáḥib and a direct reply would have contravened the laws of Islám. The answer was therefore sent down from the heaven of the Divine Will in an implicit manner. Indeed the statement in the first passage where He saith: "The All-Knowing Physician hath His finger on the pulse of mankind" was, and remaineth, the answer to his question. He further saith: "Be anxiously concerned with the needs of the age ye live in, and center your deliberations on its exigencies and requirements." That is, fix your gaze upon the commandments of God, for whatsoever He should ordain in this day and pronounce as lawful is indeed lawful and representeth the very truth. It is incumbent upon all to turn their gaze towards the Cause of God and to observe that which hath dawned above the horizon of His Will, since it is through the potency of His name that the banner of "He doeth what He willeth" hath been unfurled and the standard of "He ordaineth what He pleaseth" hath been raised aloft. For instance, were He to pronounce water itself to be unlawful, it would indeed become unlawful, and the converse holdeth equally true. For upon no thing hath it been inscribed "this is lawful" or "this is unlawful"; nay rather, whatsoever hath been or will be revealed is by virtue of the Word of God, exalted be His glory.

These matters are sufficiently clear and require no further elaboration. Even so, certain groups believe that all the ordi-

3.31

3.32

nances current amongst them are unalterable, that they have ever been valid, and that they will forever remain so. Consider a further passage, glorified and exalted be He: "These words are being uttered in due measure, that the newly born may thrive and the tender shoot flourish. Milk must be given in suitable proportion, that the children of the world may attain to the station of maturity and abide in the court of oneness."[13] For instance, some believe that wine hath ever been and shall remain forbidden. Now, were one to inform them that it might one day be made lawful, they would arise in protest and opposition. In truth, the people of the world have yet not grasped the meaning of "He doeth whatsoever He willeth," nor have they comprehended the significance of Supreme Infallibility. The suckling child must be nourished with milk. If it be given meat it will assuredly perish, and this would be naught but sheer injustice and unwisdom. Blessed are they that understand. Supreme Infallibility, as I once heard from His blessed lips, is reserved exclusively to the Manifestations of the Cause of God and the Exponents of His Revelation. This matter is mentioned but briefly, for time is short and as scarce as the legendary phoenix.

3.33   Yet another question: "According to the teachings of the Mahábád and Hindu religions, should a person of whatever faith or nation, of whatever color, appearance, character or condition, be disposed to associate with you, ye should show forth kindness and treat him as a brother. But in other religions this is not so: their followers ill-treat and oppress the adherents of other faiths, consider their persecution as an act of worship, and regard their kindred and their possessions as lawful unto themselves. Which approach is acceptable in the sight of God?"

The former statement hath ever been and will continue to 3.34
be true. It is not permissible to contend with anyone, nor is
it acceptable in the sight of God to ill-treat or oppress any
soul. Time and again have these sublime words streamed
from the Pen of the Most High, blessed and exalted be He:
"O ye children of men! The fundamental purpose animat-
ing the Faith of God and His Religion is to safeguard the
interests and promote the unity of the human race, and to
foster the spirit of love and fellowship amongst men. Suffer
it not to become a source of dissension and discord, of hate
and enmity." This subject hath already been set forth and
explained in various Tablets.

It behooveth him who expoundeth the Word of God to 3.35
deliver it with the utmost good-will, kindness, and compassion. As to him that embraceth the truth and is honored
with recognizing Him, his name shall be recorded in the
Crimson Book among the inmates of the all-highest Paradise. Should a soul fail, however, to accept the truth, it
is in no wise permissible to contend with him. In another
connection He saith: "Blessed and happy is he that ariseth
to promote the best interests of the peoples and kindreds of
the earth." Likewise He saith: "The people of Bahá should
soar high above the peoples of the world." In matters of religion every form of fanaticism, hatred, dissension and strife
is strictly forbidden.

In this day a Luminary hath dawned above the horizon of 3.36
divine providence, upon whose brow the Pen of Glory hath
inscribed these exalted words: "We have called you into being
to show forth love and fidelity, not animosity and hatred."
Likewise, on another occasion, He—exalted and glorified be
His name—hath revealed the following words in the Persian

tongue, words through which the hearts of the well-favored and the sincere amongst His servants are consumed, the manifold pursuits of men are harmonized, and mankind is illumined by the light of divine unity and enabled to turn towards the Dayspring of divine knowledge: "The incomparable Friend saith: The path to freedom hath been outstretched; hasten ye thereunto. The wellspring of wisdom is overflowing; quaff ye therefrom. Say: O well-beloved ones! The tabernacle of unity hath been raised; regard ye not one another as strangers. Ye are the fruits of one tree, and the leaves of one branch."[14]

3.37   Justice, which consisteth in rendering each his due, dependeth upon and is conditioned by two words: reward and punishment. From the standpoint of justice, every soul should receive the reward of his actions, inasmuch as the peace and prosperity of the world depend thereon, even as He saith, exalted be His glory: "The structure of world stability and order hath been reared upon, and will continue to be sustained by, the twin pillars of reward and punishment." In brief, every circumstance requireth a different utterance and every occasion calleth for a different course of action. Blessed are they that have arisen to serve God, who speak forth wholly for His sake, and who return unto Him.

3.38   Another of his questions: "Hindus and Zoroastrians do not admit or welcome outsiders who wish to join their ranks. Christians welcome those who decide of their own accord to embrace their religion, but make no effort and exert no pressure to this end. Muslims and Jews, however, insist upon it, enjoin it upon others, and, should anyone refuse, grow hostile and regard it as lawful to seize his kindred and possessions. Which approach is acceptable in the sight of God?"

The children of men are all brothers, and the prerequi- 3.39
sites of brotherhood are manifold. Among them is that one
should wish for one's brother that which one wisheth for
oneself. Therefore, it behooveth him who is the recipient
of an inward or outward gift or who partaketh of the bread
of heaven to inform and invite his friends with the utmost
love and kindness. If they respond favorably, his object is
attained; otherwise he should leave them to themselves without contending with them or uttering a word that would
cause the least sadness. This is the undoubted truth, and
aught else is unworthy and unbecoming.

The distinguished Ṣáḥib, may God graciously aid him, 3.40
hath written that the Hindus and Zoroastrians do not per-
mit or welcome outsiders who wish to join their ranks. This
runneth counter to the purpose underlying the advent of the
Messengers of God and to that which hath been revealed in
their Books. For those Who have appeared at God's behest
have been entrusted with the guidance and education of all
people. How could they debar a seeker from the object of
his quest, or forbid a wayfarer from the desire of his heart?
The fire-temples of the world stand as eloquent testimony to
this truth. In their time they summoned, with burning zeal,
all the inhabitants of the earth to Him Who is the Spirit of
purity.

He hath moreover written that Christians welcome those 3.41
who decide of their own accord to embrace their religion,
but make no effort and exert no pressure to this end. This,
however, is a misconception. For the Christians have exerted
and continue to exert the utmost effort in teaching their
faith. Their church organizations have an expenditure of
about thirty million. Their missionaries have scattered far

and wide throughout the globe and are assiduously engaged in teaching Christianity. Thus have they compassed the world. How numerous the schools and churches they have founded to instruct children, yet their unavowed aim is that these children, as they acquire an education, may also become acquainted in their early years with the Gospel of Jesus Christ, and that the unsullied mirrors of their hearts may thus reflect that which their teachers have purposed. Indeed the followers of no other religion are as intent upon the propagation of their faith as the Christians.

3.42   In brief, what is right and true in this day and acceptable before His Throne is that which was mentioned at the outset. All men have been called into being for the betterment of the world. It behooveth every soul to arise and serve his brethren for the sake of God. Should a brother of his embrace the truth, he should rejoice that the latter hath attained unto everlasting favor. Otherwise he should implore God to guide him without manifesting the least trace of animosity or ill-feeling towards him. The reins of command are in the grasp of God. He doeth what He willeth and ordaineth as He pleaseth. He, verily, is the Almighty, the All-Praised.

3.43   We beseech the one true God, magnified be His glory, to enable us to recognize Him Whose unerring wisdom pervadeth all things and that we may acknowledge His truth. For once one hath recognized Him and borne witness to His Reality, one will no longer be troubled by the idle fancies and vain imaginings of men. The divine Physician hath the pulse of mankind within His almighty grasp. At one time He may well deem fit to sever certain infected limbs, that the disease may not spread to other parts of the body. This would be the very essence of mercy and compassion, and to none is given the right to object, for He is indeed the All-Knowing, the All-Seeing.

Another of his questions: "In the Mahábád and Zoroas- 3.44 trian religions it is said: 'Our faith and religion is superior to every other. The other Prophets and the religions they have instituted are true, but they occupy different stations before God, even as, in the court of a king, there is a gradation of ranks from the prime minister to the common soldier. Whosoever wisheth, let him keep the precepts of his religion.' Nor do they impose upon any soul. The Hindus claim that whosoever partaketh of meat, for whatever reason or under whatever circumstances, shall never catch a glimpse of Paradise. The followers of Muḥammad, Jesus and Moses maintain that a similar fate awaiteth those who fail to bear allegiance to their religions. Which belief is favored by God, glorified be His mention?"

Regarding their statement that "our faith and religion is 3.45 superior to every other," by this is meant such Prophets as have appeared before them. Viewed from one perspective these holy Souls are one: the first among them is the same as the last, and the last is the same as the first. All have proceeded from God, unto Him have they summoned all men, and unto Him have they returned. This theme hath been set forth in the Book of Certitude, which is indeed the cynosure of all books, and which streamed from the Pen of Glory in the early years of this Most Great Revelation. Blessed is he that hath beheld it and pondered its contents for the love of God, the Lord of creation.

Concerning the remark attributed to the Hindus that 3.46 whosoever partaketh of meat shall never catch a glimpse of Paradise, this runneth counter to their other assertion that all the Prophets are true. For if their truth be established, then it is absurd to claim that their followers will not ascend unto Paradise. One fain would ask what they intend by Paradise and what they have grasped thereof. In this day whosoever attaineth the good pleasure of the one true God, magnified be His glory, shall be remembered and accounted among the inmates of the all-highest Heaven and the most exalted Paradise, and shall partake of its benefits in all the worlds of God. By Him Who is the Desire of all men! The pen is powerless to portray this station or to expound this theme. How great the blessedness of him who hath attained unto the good-pleasure of God, and woe betide the heedless! Once the validity of a divinely appointed Prophet hath been established, to none is given the right to ask why or wherefore. Rather is it incumbent upon all to accept and obey whatsoever He saith. This is that which God hath decreed in all His Books, Scriptures and Tablets.

3.47   A further question that he hath asked: "The Hindus assert that God fashioned the Intellect in the form of a man named Brahma, Who came into this world and was the cause of its progress and development, and that all Hindus are His descendants. The followers of Zoroaster say: 'God, through the agency of the Primal Intellect, created a man whose name is Mahábád and who is our ancestor.' They believe the modes of creation to be six in number. Two were mentioned above; the others are creation from water, earth, fire, and from bears and monkeys. The Hindus and Zoroastrians both say that they are begotten of the Intellect, and thus do not admit others into their folds. Are these assertions true or not? That wise Master is requested to indicate that which he deemeth appropriate."

The entire creation hath been called into being through 3.48
the Will of God, magnified be His glory, and peerless
Adam hath been fashioned through the agency of His all-
compelling Word, a Word which is the source, the wellspring,
the repository, and the dawning-place of the intellect. From
it all creation hath proceeded, and it is the channel of God's
primal grace. None can grasp the reality of the origin of
creation save God, exalted be His glory, Whose knowledge
embraceth all things both before and after they come into
being. Creation hath neither beginning nor end, and none
hath ever unraveled its mystery. Its knowledge hath ever
been, and shall remain, hidden and preserved with those
Who are the Repositories of divine knowledge.

The world of existence is contingent, inasmuch as it is 3.49
preceded by a cause, while essential preexistence hath ever
been, and shall remain, confined to God, magnified be His
glory. This statement is being made lest one be inclined to
conclude from the earlier assertion, namely that creation
hath no beginning and no end, that it is preexistent. True
and essential preexistence is exclusively reserved to God,
while the preexistence of the world is secondary and relative.
All that hath been inferred about firstness, lastness and such
hath in truth been derived from the sayings of the Prophets,
Apostles, and chosen Ones of God.

As to the "realm of subtle entities"[15] which is often referred 3.50
to, it pertaineth to the Revelation of the Prophets, and aught
else is mere superstition and idle fancy. At the time of the
Revelation all men are equal in rank. By reason, however, of
their acceptance or rejection, rise or fall, motion or stillness,
recognition or denial, they come to differ thereafter. For
instance, the one true God, magnified be His glory, speak-

ing through the intermediary of His Manifestation, doth ask: "Am I not your Lord?" Every soul that answereth "Yea, verily!" is accounted among the most distinguished of all men in the sight of God. Our meaning is that ere the Word of God is delivered, all men are deemed equal in rank and their station is one and the same. It is only thereafter that differences appear, as thou hast no doubt observed.

3.51   It is clearly established from that which hath been mentioned that none may ever justifiably claim: "We are begotten of the Intellect, while all others stem from another origin." The truth that shineth bright and resplendent as the sun is this, that all have been created through the operation of the Divine Will and have proceeded from the same source, that all are from Him and that unto Him they shall all return. This is the meaning of that blessed verse in the Qur'án which hath issued from the Pen of the All-Merciful: "Verily, we are God's, and to Him shall we return."[16]

3.52   As is clear and evident to thee, the answer to all of the questions mentioned above was embodied in but one of the passages revealed by the Pen of the Most High. Blessed are they who, freed from worldly matters and sanctified from idle fancies and vain imaginings, traverse the meads of divine knowledge and discern in all things the tokens of His glory.

3.53   Numerous passages have been revealed in the name of his honor the Ṣáḥib. Were he to appreciate their value and avail himself of their fruits, he would experience such joy that all the sorrows of the world would be powerless to afflict him. God grant that he may be enabled to sincerely voice, and to act in accordance with, the following words: "Say: It is God; then leave them to entertain themselves with their cavilings."[17] May he endeavor to guide those deprived souls who remain secluded in darkness and obscurity towards the light of the Sun. May he seize, through the potency of the Most Great Name, the banner that speaketh of naught save His Revelation and march at the forefront of the people of the former religions, that perchance the darkness of the world may be dispelled and the effulgent rays of the Sun of Truth may shine upon all mankind. This, in truth, is the most perfect bounty and the highest calling. Should man fail to attain unto this sublime station, where then can he find comfort and joy? What will sustain and animate him? With whom will he commune at the hour of repose, and whose name will he invoke when he riseth from slumber? Again: "Verily, we are God's, and to Him shall we return."

His last question. "Most of the Tablets that we have seen 3.54 are in Arabic. However, since the Beloved in this age is of Persian descent, the Arabic tongue should be abandoned and discarded. For to this day the Arabs themselves have not understood the meaning of the Qur'án, whereas the Persian language is highly prized, lauded and admired among the dwellers of the inhabited quarter of the globe. And just as the Persian of the present day is superior to Arabic, so too is Old Persian, which is greatly favored by the people of India and others. It would therefore be preferable if the words of God, magnified be His mention, were hereafter mainly delivered in pure Persian, since it attracteth the hearts to a greater degree. It is moreover requested that the reply to these questions be graciously written in pure Persian."

The Persian tongue is in truth exceedingly sweet and 3.55 pleasing, and ever since this request was submitted in His most blessed and exalted court, numerous Tablets have been revealed in that language. As to the statement concerning the

Qur'án implying that its outward meaning hath not been understood, in reality it hath been interpreted in numerous ways and translated into countless languages. That which men have been unable to grasp are its hidden mysteries and inner meanings. And all that they have said or will say is limited in scope and should be seen as commensurate with their rank and station. For none can fathom its true meaning save God, the One, the Incomparable, the All-Knowing.

3.56   In this day He Who is the Lord, the Ruler, the Fashioner, and the Refuge of the world hath appeared. Let every ear be eager to hearken unto that which will be revealed from the kingdom of His will; let every eye be expectant to gaze upon that which will shine forth from the Daystar of knowledge and wisdom. By Him Who is the Desire of the world! This is the day for eyes to see and for ears to hear, for hearts to perceive and for tongues to speak forth. Blessed are they that have attained thereunto; blessed are they that have sought after and recognized it! This is the day whereon every man may accede unto everlasting honor, for whatsoever hath streamed forth from the Pen of Glory in regard to any soul is adorned with the ornament of immortality. Again, blessed are they that have attained thereunto!

3.57   The distinguished Ṣáḥib hath written: "Since the Beloved in this age is of Persian descent, the Arabic tongue should be abandoned and discarded." In this connection these sublime words issued from the Pen of the Most High, magnified and exalted be His glory: "Both Arabic and Persian are laudable. That which is desired of a language is that it convey the intent of the speaker, and either language can serve this purpose. And since in this day the Orb of knowledge hath risen in the firmament of Persia, this tongue deserveth every praise."

The light of truth is indeed shining resplendent above 3.58
the horizon of divine utterance, and hence no further elaboration is required from this evanescent soul or from others like unto him. Although there can be no question or doubt as to the sweetness of the Persian tongue, yet it hath not the scope of the Arabic. There are many things which have not been expressed in Persian, that is to say, words referring to such things have not been devised, whilst in Arabic there are several words describing the same thing. Indeed there existeth no language in the world as vast and comprehensive as Arabic. This statement is prompted by truth and fairness; otherwise it is clear that in this day the world is being illumined by the splendors of that Sun which hath dawned above the horizon of Persia, and that the merits of this sweet language can scarcely be overestimated.

All the questions of his honor the Ṣáhib have herewith 3.59
been mentioned and duly answered. If it be deemed appropriate and advisable, there would be no harm in his perusing these answers himself, and likewise they may be read by the beloved friends in that land, such as Jináb-i-'Alí-Akbar, upon him be the glory of God, the Supreme Ordainer, and Jináb-i-Áqá Mírzá Asadu'lláh, upon him be the Glory of Glories.

This servant beseecheth the one True God exalted be 3.60
His glory—to graciously adorn the world of humanity with justice and fairmindedness, although in truth the latter is but one of the expressions of the former. Verily, justice is a lamp that guideth man aright amidst the darkness of the world and shieldeth him from every danger. It is indeed a shining lamp. God grant that the rulers of the earth may be illumined by its light. This servant further imploreth God

to graciously aid all men to do His will and pleasure. He, in truth, is the Lord of this world and of the world to come. No God is there but Him, the Almighty, the Most-Powerful.

4
TABLET OF THE SEVEN QUESTIONS
(LAWḤ-I-HAFT PURSISH)

IN THE NAME OF THE LORD OF UTTERANCE, THE ALL-WISE

All praise be to the sanctified Lord Who hath illumined the world through the splendors of the Daystar of His grace. From the letter "B" He hath made the Most Great Ocean to appear, and from the letter "H" He hath caused His inmost Essence to be made manifest. He is that Almighty One Whose purpose the might of men can never hope to frustrate and the flow of Whose utterance the hosts of kings are powerless to halt.

4.1

Thy letter was received, and We perused it and heard thy call. Within it were enshrined the precious pearls of love and the hidden mysteries of affection. We beseech the peerless Lord to enable thee to assist His Cause and to lead those who are sore athirst in the wilderness of ignorance to the water of life. His might, in truth, is equal to all things. That which thou didst ask of the Ocean of Knowledge and the Orb of Insight hath met with His acceptance.

4.2

The first question: "In what tongue and towards what direction doth it behoove us to worship the one true God?"

4.3

The beginning of all utterance is the worship of God, and this followeth upon His recognition. Sanctified must be the eye if it is to truly recognize Him, and sanctified must be the tongue if it is to befittingly utter His praise. In this

4.4

Day the faces of the people of insight and understanding are turned in His direction; nay every direction inclineth itself towards Him. O lion-hearted one! We beseech God that thou mayest become a champion in this arena, arise with heavenly power and say: "O high priests! Ears have been given you that they may hearken unto the mystery of Him Who is the Self-Dependent, and eyes that they may behold Him. Wherefore flee ye? The Incomparable Friend is manifest. He speaketh that wherein lieth salvation. Were ye, O high priests, to discover the perfume of the rose garden of understanding, ye would seek none other but Him, and would recognize, in His new vesture, the All-Wise and Peerless One, and would turn your eyes from the world and all who seek it, and would arise to help Him."

4.5 The second question concerneth faith and religion. The Faith of God hath in this Day been made manifest. He Who is the Lord of the world is come and hath shown the way. His faith is the faith of benevolence and His religion is the religion of forbearance. This faith bestoweth eternal life and this religion enableth mankind to dispense with all else. It verily embraceth all faiths and all religions. Take hold thereof and guard it well.

4.6 The third question: "In what manner shall we deal with the people of this age, who have each chosen to follow a different religion and who each regard their own faith and religion as excelling and surpassing all the others, that we may be shielded from the onslaught of their words and deeds?"

4.7 O lion-hearted one amongst men! Regard the afflictions endured in the path of God as comfort itself. Every affliction suffered for His sake is a potent remedy, every bitterness is naught but sweetness and every abasement an exaltation.

Were men to apprehend and acknowledge this truth, they would readily lay down their lives for such affliction. For it is the key to inestimable treasures, and no matter how outwardly abhorrent, it hath ever been and will continue to be inwardly prized. We accept and affirm what thou hast said, for the people of the world are indeed bereft of the light of the Orb of justice and regard it as their enemy.

If thou desirest to be freed from affliction, recite thou this prayer which hath been revealed by the Pen of the All-Merciful: "O God, my God! I testify to Thy unity and to Thy oneness. I beseech Thee, O Thou Possessor of names and Fashioner of the heavens, by the pervasive influence of Thine exalted Word and the potency of Thy supreme Pen, to aid me with the ensigns of Thy power and might, and to protect me from the mischief of Thine enemies who have violated Thy Covenant and Thy Testament. Thou art, verily, the Almighty, the Most Powerful." This invocation is an impregnable stronghold and an indomitable army. It conferreth protection and ensureth deliverance. 4.8

The fourth question: "Our Books have announced that Sháh Bahrám will come, invested with manifold signs, to guide the people aright. . . ." 4.9

O friend! Whatsoever hath been announced in the Books hath been revealed and made clear. From every side the signs have been manifested. The Omnipotent One is calling, in this Day, and announcing the appearance of the Supreme Heaven. The world hath been illumined with the splendors of His revelation, yet how few are the eyes that can behold it! Beseech the peerless and incomparable Lord to bestow a penetrating insight upon His servants, for insight leadeth to true knowledge and is conducive to salvation. Indeed, the 4.10

attainments of man's understanding are dependent upon his keenness of sight. Were the children of men to gaze with the eye of understanding, they would see the world illumined with a new light in this Day. Say: The Daystar of knowledge is manifest and the Luminary of insight hath appeared. Fortunate indeed is the one who hath attained, who hath witnessed, and who hath recognized.

4.11   The fifth question concerneth the bridge of Ṣirát, Paradise, and Hell. The Prophets of God have come in truth and have spoken the truth. Whatsoever the Messenger of God hath announced hath been and will be made manifest. The world is established upon the foundations of reward and punishment. Knowledge and understanding have ever affirmed and will continue to affirm the reality of Paradise and Hell, for reward and punishment require their existence. Paradise signifieth first and foremost the good-pleasure of God. Whosoever attaineth His good-pleasure is reckoned and recorded among the inhabitants of the most exalted paradise and will attain, after the ascension of his soul, that which pen and ink are powerless to describe. For them that are endued with insight and have fixed their gaze upon the Most Sublime Vision, the Bridge, the Balance, Paradise, Hellfire, and all that hath been mentioned and recorded in the Sacred Scriptures are clear and manifest. At the time of the appearance and manifestation of the rays of the Daystar of Truth, all occupy the same station. God then proclaimeth that which He willeth, and whoso heareth His call and acknowledgeth His truth is accounted among the inhabitants of Paradise. Such a soul hath traversed the Bridge, the Balance, and all that hath been recorded regarding the Day of Resurrection, and hath reached his destination. The Day of God's Revelation is the Day of the most great Resurrection. We cherish the hope that, quaffing from the choice wine of divine inspiration and the pure waters of heavenly grace, thou mayest attain the station of discovery and witnessing, and behold, both outwardly and inwardly, all that which thou hast mentioned.

The sixth question: "After relinquishing the body, that is to say, after the soul hath been separated from the body, it hasteneth to the abode hereafter. . . ." 4.12

In reference to this theme there appeared some time past from the Pen of divine knowledge that which sufficeth the men of insight and imparteth the greatest joy to the people of understanding. Verily, We say: The soul is gladdened by goodly deeds and profiteth from the contributions made in the path of God. 4.13

The seventh question regardeth the name, lineage, and ancestry of the Holy One.* Abu'l-Faḍl-i-Gulpáygání, upon him be My glory, hath written in this regard, based on the Sacred Scriptures, that which bestoweth knowledge and increaseth understanding. 4.14

The Faith of God is endowed with penetrating might and power. Erelong that which hath flowed from Our tongue will outwardly come to pass. We beseech God to bestow upon thee the strength to assist Him. He, verily, is the All-Knowing, the All-Powerful. Wert thou to obtain and peruse the Súriy-i-Ra'ís and the Súriy-i-Mulúk, thou wouldst find thyself able to dispense with thy questions and wouldst arise to serve the 4.15

---

* Bahá'u'lláh

Cause of God in such wise that the oppression of the world and the onslaught of its peoples would fail to deter thee from aiding Him Who is the ancient and sovereign Lord of all.

4.16   We implore God to confirm thee in that which will exalt and immortalize thy name. Make thou an effort, that haply thou mayest obtain the aforementioned Tablets and acquire therefrom a share of the pearls of wisdom and utterance that have issued from the treasury of the Pen of the All-Merciful. The glory of God rest upon thee, upon every steadfast and unwavering heart and upon every constant and faithful soul.

5
TWO OTHER TABLETS

THE BEGINNING OF ALL UTTERANCE
IS THE PRAISE OF GOD

O servants! The wellsprings of divine bestowal are streaming 5.1
forth. Quaff ye therefrom, that by the aid of the incomparable Friend ye may be sanctified from this darksome world
of dust and enter His abode. Renounce the world and direct
your steps toward the city of the Beloved.

O servants! The fire that consumeth all veils hath been 5.2
kindled by My hand; quench it not with the waters of
ignorance. The heavens are the token of My greatness; look
upon them with a pure eye. The stars bear witness to My
truth; bear ye likewise witness thereto.

O servants! Eyes are needed if one is to see, and ears, if 5.3
one is to hear. Whoso in this blessed Day hath not heard
the divine call hath indeed no ear. By this is not meant that
bodily ear that is perceived by the eye. Open your inner eye,
that ye may behold the celestial Fire, and listen with the ear
of inner understanding, that ye may hear the delightsome
words of the Beloved.

O servants! If your heart acheth for the Beloved, lo, the 5.4
remedy is come! If ye have eyes to see, behold, the shining
countenance of the Friend hath appeared! Kindle ye the fire
of knowledge and flee from the ignorant. Such are the words
of the Lord of the world.

5.5   O servants! Lifeless is the body that is bereft of a soul, and withered the heart that is devoid of the remembrance of its Lord. Commune with the remembrance of the Friend and shun the enemy. Your enemy is such things as ye have acquired of your own inclination, to which ye have firmly clung, and whereby ye have sullied your souls. The soul hath been created for the remembrance of the Friend; safeguard its purity. The tongue hath been created to bear witness to God; pollute it not with the mention of the wayward.

5.6   O servants! Verily I say, he is to be accounted as truthful who hath beheld the straight Path. That Path is one, and God hath chosen and prepared it. It shineth as resplendent amongst all paths as the sun amongst the stars. Whosoever hath not attained it hath failed to apprehend the truth and hath gone astray. Such are the counsels of the incomparable, the peerless Lord.

5.7   O servants! This nether world is the abode of demons: Guard yourselves from approaching them. By demons is meant those wayward souls who, with the burden of their evil deeds, slumber in the chambers of oblivion. Their sleep is preferable to their wakefulness, and their death is better than their life.

5.8   O servants! Not every mortal frame hath a spirit or is imbued with life. In this day he is endowed with spirit who with all his heart seeketh the abode of the Beloved. The end of all beginnings is to be found in this Day: Turn ye not a blind eye unto it. The matchless Friend is nigh: Stray not far from Him.

5.9   O servants! Ye are even as saplings in a garden, which are near to perishing for want of water. Wherefore, revive your souls with the heavenly water that is raining down from the clouds of divine bounty. Words must be followed by deeds. Whoso accepteth the words of the Friend is in truth a man of deeds; otherwise a dead carcass is verily of greater worth.

O servants! Pleasant is the utterance of the Friend: Where is the soul who will taste its sweetness, and where is the ear that will hearken unto it? Well is it with him who, in this Day, communeth with the Friend and in His path renounceth and forsaketh all save Him, that he may behold a new world and gain admittance to the everlasting paradise. 5.10

The Lord of the world saith: O servants! Forsake your own desires and seek that which I have desired for you. Walk ye not without one to guide you on the way, and accept ye not the words of every guide. How numerous the guides who have gone astray and failed to discover the straight path! He alone is a guide who is free from the bondage of this world and whom nothing whatsoever can deter from speaking the truth. 5.11

O servants! Follow the path of truthfulness and turn not away from the needy. Make mention of Me before the great ones of the earth and fear not. 5.12

O servants! Be pure in your deeds, and conduct yourselves in accordance with the words of God. Such are the counsels of the incomparable Lord. 5.13

THE BEGINNING OF EVERY ACCOUNT
IS THE NAME OF GOD

O friends of God! Incline your inner ears to the voice of the 6.1
peerless and self-subsisting Lord, that He may deliver you
from the bonds of entanglement and the depths of darkness and enable you to attain the eternal light. Ascent and
descent, stillness and motion, have come into being through
the will of the Lord of all that hath been and shall be. The
cause of ascent is lightness, and the cause of lightness is
heat. Thus hath it been decreed by God. The cause of stillness is weight and density, which in turn are caused by cold.
Thus hath it been decreed by God.

And since He hath ordained heat to be the source of 6.2
motion and ascent and the cause of attainment to the
desired goal, He hath therefore kindled with the mystic
hand that Fire that dieth not and sent it forth into the world,
that this divine Fire might, by the heat the love of God,
guide and attract all mankind to the abode of the incomparable Friend. This is the mystery enshrined in your Book
that was sent down aforetime, a mystery which hath until
now remained concealed from the eyes and hearts of men.
That primal Fire hath in this Day appeared with a new radiance and with immeasurable heat. This divine Fire burneth
of itself, with neither fuel nor fume, that it might draw away

such excess moisture and cold as are the cause of torpor and weariness, of lethargy and despondency, and lead the entire creation to the court of the presence of the All-Merciful. Whoso hath approached this Fire hath been set aflame and attained the desired goal, and whoso hath removed himself therefrom hath remained deprived.

6.3   O servant of God! Turn thou away from the stranger, that thou mayest recognize the Friend. He indeed is a stranger who leadeth you away from the Friend. This is not the day whereon the high priests can command and exercise their authority. In your Book it is stated that the high priests will, on that Day, lead men far astray, and will prevent them from drawing nigh unto Him. He indeed is a high priest who hath seen the light and hastened unto the way leading to the Beloved. Such a man is a benevolent priest and a source of illumination to the whole world.

6.4   O servant of God! Any priest who leadeth thee away from this Fire, which is the reality of the Light and the mystery of divine Revelation, is indeed thine enemy. Suffer not the words of the foe to hold thee back from the Friend or the insinuations of the enemy to cause thee to forsake the Beloved.

6.5   O servant of God! The day of deeds hath come: Now is not the time for words. The Messenger of God hath appeared: Now is not the hour for hesitation. Open thine inner eye that thou mayest behold the face of the Beloved, and hearken with thine inner ear that thou mayest hear the sweet murmur of His celestial voice.

6.6   O servant of God! The robe of divine bestowal hath been sewn and readied. Take hold of it and attire thyself therewith. Renounce and forsake the people of the world. O wise one! Shouldst thou heed the counsel of thy Lord, thou wouldst be released from the bondage of His servants and behold thyself exalted above all men.

O servant of God! We have bestowed a dewdrop from the ocean of divine grace; would that men might drink therefrom! We have brought a trace of the sweet melodies of the Beloved; would that men might hearken with their inner ear! Soar upon the wings of joy in the atmosphere of the love of God. Regard the people of the world as dead and seek the fellowship of the living. Whoso hath not breathed the sweet fragrance of the Beloved at this dawntide is indeed accounted among the dead. He Who is the All-Sufficing proclaimeth aloud: "The realm of joy hath been ushered in; be not sorrowful! The hidden mystery hath been made manifest; be not disheartened!" Wert thou to apprehend the surpassing greatness of this Day, thou wouldst renounce the world and all that dwell therein and hasten unto the way that leadeth to the Lord. 6.7

O servants of God! Deprived souls are heedless of this triumphant Day, and chilled hearts have no share of the heat of this blazing Fire. 6.8

O servant of God! The Tree which We had planted with the Hand of Providence hath borne its destined fruit, and the glad-tidings We had imparted in the Book have appeared in full effect. 6.9

O servant of God! We revealed Ourself to thee once in thy sleep, but thou didst remain unaware. Remember now, that thou mayest perceive and hasten with heart and soul to the placeless Friend. 6.10

O servant of God! Say: O high priests! The Hand of Omnipotence is stretched forth from behind the clouds; 6.11

behold ye it with new eyes. The tokens of His majesty and greatness are unveiled; gaze ye on them with pure eyes.

6.12   O servant of God! The Daystar of the everlasting realm is shining resplendent above the horizon of His will and the Oceans of divine bounty are surging. Bereft indeed is the one who hath failed to behold them, and lifeless the one who hath not attained thereunto. Close thine eyes to this nether world, open them to the countenance of the incomparable Friend, and commune intimately with His Spirit.

6.13   O servant of God! With a pure heart unloose thy tongue in the praise of thy Lord for having made mention of thee through His gem-scattering pen. Couldst thou but realize the greatness of this bestowal, thou wouldst find thyself invested with everlasting life.

NOTES

Introduction
1. Shoghi Effendi, *God Passes By,* p. 110.
2. Bahá'u'lláh, The Kitáb-i-Íqán, ¶24.

Gems of Divine Mysteries
1. Cf. Qur'án 67:3.
2. Cf. Qur'án 24:35.
3. Matt. 24:19.
4. Cf. Matt. 24:29–31.
5. Mark 13:19.
6. Cf. Luke 21:25–28.
7. John 15:26–27.
8. John 14:26.
9. John 16:5–6.
10. John 16:7.
11. John 16:13.
12. The Imáms of Shí'ih Islám.
13. Cf. Matt. 24:35; Mark 13:31; Luke 21:33.
14. The Antichrist, who it was believed would appear at the advent of the Promised One, to contend with and be ultimately defeated by Him.

15. Another figure who it was believed would raise the banner of rebellion between Mecca and Damascus at the appearance of the Promised One.

16. Qur'án 16:43.

17. A magician in the court of Pharaoh during the time of Moses.

18. Qur'án 83:6; 2:89.

19. The Imáms of Shí'ih Islám.

20. Qur'án 29:2.

21. Qur'án 2:156.

22. Qur'án 29:69.

23. Qur'án 2:282.

24. From a Hadíth.

25. Ibid.

26. Qur'án 30:30.

27. Qur'án 48:23.

28. Qur'án 67:3.

29. Qur'án 17:110.

30. Qur'án 57:3.

31. The twelfth Imám, Muḥammad al-Mahdí, the son of Ḥasan al-'Askarí.

32. According to Shí'ih traditions, the twin cities of Jábul-qá and Jábulṣá are the dwelling place of the Hidden Imám (the Promised One), whence He will appear on the Day of Resurrection.

33. Qur'án 33:40.

34. Qur'án 13:2.

35. Qur'án 74:50.

36. Cf. Qur'án 13:5.

37. Qur'án 11:7.

38. Qur'án 3:185.

39. Qur'án 16:97.

40. Qur'án 3:169.

41. From a Ḥadíth.

42. Qur'án 7:179.

43. Cf. Qur'án 9:109; 3:103.

44. Qur'án 6:122.

45. John 3:5–7.

46. Cf. Rev. 1:14–16; 2:18; 19:15.

47. Cf. Qur'án 80:41; 83:24.

48. Qur'án 11:112.

49. Cf. Luke 12:53.

50. Cf. Qur'án 1:4.

51. Qur'án 14:48.

52. Qur'án 14:5.

53. Cf. Qur'án 21:23.

54. From a saying of Imám 'Alí.

55. From the *Díván* of Ibn-i-Fáriḍ.

56. Ibid.

57. Cf. Qur'án 10:61; 34:3.

58. From a Ḥadíth.

59. From the *Díván* of Ibn-i-Fáriḍ.

60. Cf. Qur'án 39:10.

61. Qur'án 2:156.

62. Qur'án 4:130.

63. Cf. Qur'án 50:30.

Tablet to Mánikchí Ṣáḥib

1. For forty years, Bahá'u'lláh suffered a series of imprisonments and exiles that lasted until His passing in 1892. At the time this Tablet was written, He was confined in the prison-city of Akká, in what is now northern Israel. He often

referred to it in His writings as "The Most Great Prison."

2. From the Lawḥ-i-Maqṣúd; cf. Bahá'u'lláh, *Tablets of Bahá'u'lláh,* p. 171.

3. Ibid., p. 169.

Responses to questions of Mánikchí Ṣáḥib from a Tablet to Mírzá Abu'l-Faḍl

1. Qur'án 3:1.

2. Qur'án 2:285.

3. Qur'án 2:253.

4. See 2.4.

5. The "Necessary Being" (*vájibu'l-vujúd*) refers to God; this term was used by Muslim philosophers such as al-Farabi and can be traced to Aristotle.

6. *Taqvá,* translated here as "righteousness," has further connotations of piety, fear of God, and right conduct that cannot all be conveyed with a single word in English.

7. In Islamic law, religious principles (*uṣúl*; lit. "roots"), concern the sources of the law that can be explicitly derived from the Qur'án and the Ḥadíth, whereas secondary laws and ordinances (*furú'*, lit. "branches") are deduced from the former through the discipline of jurisprudence (*fiqh*).

8. Possible reference to Qur'án 2:187, which contains instructions regarding the Fast: "Eat and drink until ye can discern a white thread from a black thread by the daybreak." (Rodwell trans.)

9. Qur'án 6:91.

10. Among the rites performed by Muslim pilgrims during the hajj.

11. See 1.14.

12. Qur'án 2:143.

13. See 1.18.

14. See 1.15.

15. The "realm of subtle entities" ('álam-i-dharr) is an allusion to the Covenant between God and Adam mentioned in Qur'án 7:172. In a Tablet, 'Abdu'l-Bahá has written, "The realm of subtle entities that is alluded to referreth to the realities, specifications, individuations, capacities and potentialities of man in the mirror of the divine knowledge. As these potentialities and capacities differ, they each have their own particular exigency. That exigency consisteth in acquiescence and supplication." (Má'idiy-i-Ásmání, vol. 2, p. 30)

16. Qur'án 2:156.

17. Qur'án 6:91.

GLOSSARY

Abraham. Considered by Bahá'ís to be a **Manifestation of God,** He is also recognized as the founder of monotheism and the father of the Jewish and Arab peoples. **Muḥammad, the Báb,** and **Bahá'u'lláh** are among His descendants.

Abu'l-Faḍl-i-Gulpáygání. See **Mírzá Abu'l-Faḍl.**

Abú-Ḥanífih (Abu Hanifa). An eighth-century **Islámic** scholar who founded the Hanafi school of Islámic jurisprudence.

Abú-Jahl. (Lit., "Father of Folly.") The title given to an implacable enemy of the Prophet **Muḥammad.**

Adam. Considered by Bahá'ís to be the first **Manifestation of God** to have appeared in recorded religious history.

Alif. Lám. Mím. Arabic letters that appear at the head of twenty-nine súrihs (chapters) of the Qur'án.

Báb, the. (Lit., "Gate.") The title assumed by Mírzá 'Alí-Muḥammad of Shíráz (b. October 20, 1819; d. July 9,

1850) after the declaration of His mission on May 23, 1844. He is the **Qá'im** and Mihdí of **Islám** and the Forerunner of **Bahá'u'lláh.**

Bahá, people of. Followers of **Bahá'u'lláh;** Bahá'ís.

Bahá'u'lláh (Lit., "Glory of God"). Title of Mírzá Ḥusayn-'Alí (b. November 12, 1817; d. May 29, 1892), the Founder of the Bahá'í Faith.

Bedouin. Tribes of nomadic Arabs who live in the deserts of North Africa, Syria, and Arabia.

Brahma. The creator aspect of the Hindu sacred triad of gods. Brahma is portrayed as the creator of both the universe and humankind.

Chosen Ones (of God). See **Manifestations of God.**

Day of Judgment. See **Day of Resurrection.**

Day of Reckoning. See **Day of Resurrection.**

Day of Resurrection. The time of the appearance of the **Manifestation of God,** when the true character of souls is judged according to their response to His Revelation. (Also known as the Day of Judgment or the Day of Reckoning).

Dove of Holiness. A term referring to the Spirit of God that animates His Manifestations.

Evangel. Refers to the Gospel, the first four books of the New Testament.

Hajj. Pilgrimage taken by Muslims to **Mecca** at least once in a lifetime, as instituted in the Qur'án.

Ḥamzih. "The Prince of Martyrs," the title given to **Muḥammad's** uncle, 'Abdu'l-Muṭṭalib.

Ḥijáz (Hejaz). A region in northwest present-day Saudi Arabia that is known for the **Islámic** holy city of Mecca, which lies within it.

Him Whom God shall make manifest. The messianic figure anticipated in **the Báb's** writings as the one Who would come after Him and complete His mission. In 1863, **Bahá'u'lláh** declared that He was the one who had been foretold by the Báb.

Horeb. Another name for Mount **Sinai.**

Imám. Designates in its most general sense an **Islámic** religious leader who leads the prayers in the mosque and, more particularly in S͟hí'ih Islám, the twelve hereditary successors of the Prophet **Muḥammad.**

Imám 'Alí. The first **Imám,** son-in-law of **Muḥammad.**

Imám Ḥusayn. Son of 'Alí and Fáṭimih, grandson of the Prophet **Muḥammad,** and, in S͟hí'ih **Islám,** the third Imám.

Islám. (Lit., "Submission to the Will of God") The religion of **Muḥammad,** upheld by Bahá'ís as divine in origin.

Jesus. The founder of Christianity, recognized by Bahá'ís as a **Manifestation of God.** The Bahá'í writings often refer to Him as "the Spirit of God" and "the Son."

Joseph. The son of Jacob, who is mentioned in the Qur'án as an inspired prophet.

Mahábád. The first of a succession of prophets recognized in the Zoroastrian faith.

Manifestation of God. Designation of one Who is the Founder of a religious Dispensation, inasmuch as in His words, His person, and His actions He manifests the nature and purpose of God in accordance with the capacity and needs of the people to whom He comes.

Manifestation(s). See **Manifestation of God.**

Mecca. A city in Saudi Arabia that is the holy city of **Islám** and the birthplace of **Muḥammad.** It is the principal place of pilgrimage for Muslims.

Mírzá Abu'l-Faḍl. An eminent early Bahá'í, who was renowned as a scholar of both **Islám** and the Bahá'í teachings.

Moses. Founder of Judaism, regarded by Bahá'ís as a **Manifestation of God.**

Muḥammad. Prophet and Founder of **Islám.** Bahá'ís regard **Muḥammad** as a **Manifestation of God,** and His book, the Qur'án, as holy scripture.

Najaf. A city in south central Iraq considered holy by Shí'ih Muslims. It was the site of the martyrdom of the **Imám 'Alí,** the cousin of **Muḥammad,** whose shrine is a place of pilgrimage for Shí'ih Muslims.

Nimrod. A descendant of Ham represented in Genesis as a mighty hunter and a king of Shinar. According to Jewish and Islámic traditions, he persecuted **Abraham,** and his name became symbolic of great pride.

Paran. A mountain range north of **Sinai** and south of Seir; all are sacred as places of revelation.

People of Bahá. See **Bahá, people of.**

Qá'im. (Lit. "He Who Arises") In **Shí'ih Islám,** a reference to the Twelfth **Imám,** the Mihdí, who was to return in the fullness of time and bring a reign of righteousness to the world. **The Báb** declared Himself to be the Qá'im and the Gate to a greater messenger, **"Him Whom God shall make manifest."**

Qiblih. (Lit., "Point of Adoration") The focus to which the faithful turn in prayer. The Qur'án establishes the Ka'bih in Mecca as the Qiblih for Muslims. For Bahá'ís, the Qiblih is **Bahá'u'lláh's** Shrine in Bahjí, Israel.

Riḍván. The name of the custodian of Paradise. **Bahá'u'lláh** uses it to denote Paradise itself.

Seal of the Prophets. A title of **Muḥammad** referring to the close of the Prophetic Cycle.

<u>Sh</u>áh Bahrám. The world-redeeming figure prophesied in the Zoroastrian faith, Whose appearance would create an era of world peace. Bahá'ís believe this prophecy was fulfilled by **Bahá'u'lláh.**

<u>Sh</u>í'ih Islám. One of the two major branches of **Islám** (the other being Sunní). Its followers view the descendants of 'Alí, son-in-law of the Prophet **Muḥammad,** as the only rightful successors to Muḥammad.

Sinai. The mountain where God gave the tables of the Law to **Moses** (Qur'án 7:139 and Exod. 19); sometimes an emblem of the human heart, which is the place of God's descent.

Ṣiráṭ. (Lit., "path," "way") In **Islám,** the bridge leading to Paradise. According to Muslim tradition, a bridge will be extended over Hell in the Last Days, and men will have to cross over it to reach Paradise.

Supreme Infallibility. This is the infallibility of which only **Manifestations of God** are possessed. It is the station in which whatever emanates from the Manifestation of God is the unquestioned truth. Also called the Most Great Infallibility.

Súriy-i-Mulúk. Tablet revealed by **Bahá'u'lláh** in Adrianople to the kings of the world collectively. In it He boldly proclaims His station as **Manifestation of God.** [The text of this Tablet can be found in Bahá'u'lláh, *The Summons of the Lord of Hosts* (Wilmette, IL: Bahá'í Publishing, 2006), pp. 269–345.]

Súriy-i-Ra'ís. Tablet revealed by **Bahá'u'lláh** and addressed to 'Alí Páshá, the Ottoman prime minister during the time of Bahá'u'lláh. [The text of this Tablet can be found in Bahá'u'lláh, *The Summons of the Lord of Hosts* (Wilmette, IL: Bahá'í Publishing, 2006), pp. 211–35.]

Tablet. A term for a sacred epistle containing a revelation from God. The giving of the Law to **Moses** on tables, or tablets, is mentioned in Qur'án 7:142: "We wrote for him (Moses) upon tables *(alwah,* pl. of *lauh)* a monition concerning every matter." In Bahá'í scripture the term refers to letters revealed by **Bahá'u'lláh** and **the Báb.**

Torah. The Pentateuch of **Moses.**

Traditions. The authoritative record of inspired sayings and acts of **Muḥammad,** in addition to the revelation contained in the Qur'án. Often referred to individually and collectively as *hadíth.*

Zoroaster. Regarded by Bahá'ís as a **Manifestation of God** and founder of the Zoroastrian religion. He predicted the coming of a world redeemer called **Sháh-Bahrám,** Who would create an era of world peace. Bahá'ís believe the figure referred to in this prophecy is **Bahá'u'lláh,** Who is also a descendant of Zoroaster.

KEY TO PASSAGES TRANSLATED BY SHOGHI EFFENDI

Abbreviation of Sources

GWB   Bahá'u'lláh. *Gleanings from the Writings of Bahá'-u'lláh.* Wilmette: Bahá'í Publishing 2005.

KI   Bahá'u'lláh. *The Kitáb-i-Íqán.* Wilmette: Bahá'í Publishing Trust, 2003.

PDC   Shoghi Effendi. *The Promised Day Is Come.* Wilmette: Bahá'í Publishing Trust, 1996.

Paragraph	*Passage*	*Source*
2.4–2.6	"The All-Knowing Physician . . . whoso remaineth dead, shall never live."	GWB 106
2.15	"O well-beloved ones! . . . and the leaves of one branch."	GWB 112
3.5	"No distinction do We make between any of the Messengers."	KI ¶161
3.5	"Some of the Apostles We have caused to excel the others."	KI ¶110

Paragraph	Passage	Source
3.5	"The All-Knowing Physician . . . on its exigencies and requirements."	GWB 106
3.24	"We did not appoint . . . from him who turneth on his heels."	KI ¶55
3.34	"O ye children of men! . . . and discord, of hate and enmity."	GWB 110
3.35	"Blessed and happy . . . of the peoples and kindreds of the earth."	GWB 117
3.36	"O well-beloved ones! . . . and the leaves of one branch."	GWB 112
3.37	"The structure of world stability . . . reward and punishment."	GWB 112
3.51	"Verily, we are God's, and to Him shall we return."	GWB 165
3.53	"Say: It is God . . . with their cavilings."	KI ¶43
4.4	"O high priests! . . . and would arise to help Him."	PDC ¶193
4.10	"Whatsoever hath been announced . . . the Supreme Heaven."	PDC ¶193
6.3	"This is not the day . . . the way leading to the Beloved."	PDC ¶193
6.11	"O high priests! . . . gaze ye on them with pure eyes."	PDC ¶193

INDEX

BAHÁ'Í PUBLISHING
AND THE BAHÁ'Í FAITH

Bahá'í Publishing produces books based on the teachings of the Bahá'í Faith. Founded over 160 years ago, the Bahá'í Faith has spread to some 235 nations and territories and is now accepted by more than five million people. The word "Bahá'í" means "follower of Bahá'u'lláh." Bahá'u'lláh, the founder of the Bahá'í Faith, asserted that He is the Messenger of God for all of humanity in this day. The cornerstone of His teachings is the establishment of the spiritual unity of humankind, which will be achieved by personal transformation and the application of clearly identified spiritual principles. Bahá'ís also believe that there is but one religion and that all the Messengers of God—among them Abraham, Zoroaster, Moses, Krishna, Buddha, Jesus, and Muhammad—have progressively revealed its nature. Together, the world's great religions are expressions of a single, unfolding divine plan. Human beings, not God's Messengers, are the source of religious divisions, prejudices, and hatreds.

The Bahá'í Faith is not a sect or denomination of another religion, nor is it a cult or a social movement. Rather, it is a globally recognized independent world religion founded on new books of scripture revealed by Bahá'u'lláh.

Bahá'í Publishing is an imprint of the National Spiritual Assembly of the Bahá'ís of the United States.